JUNKIE MEETS JESUS IN A TRASH CAN

JUNKIE MEETS JESUS IN A TRASH CAN

Colin Garnett

Authentic

MILTON KEYNES ● COLORADO SPRINGS ● HYDERABAD

First published 2008 by Authentic Media
9 Holdom Avenue, Bletchley, Milton Keynes, MK1 1QR, UK
1820 Jet Stream Drive, Colorado Springs, CO 80921, USA
OM Authentic Media, Medchal Road, Jeedimetla Village,
Secunderabad 500 055, A.P., India
www.authenticmedia.co.uk

Authentic Media is a division of IBS-STL U.K., limited by guarantee, with its
Registered Office at Kingstown Broadway, Carlisle, Cumbria, CA3 0HA.
Registered in England & Wales No. 1216232. Registered charity 270162

British Library Cataloguing in Publication Data
A catalogue record for this book is available from the British Library

ISBN-13: 978-1-86024-720-0

Cover Design by fourninezero design.
Print Management by Adare
Printed in Great Britain by J.H. Haynes & Co., Sparkford

Contents

Contents

Chapter 1

Trapped by an Imaginary Reputation

There is a phrase in Afrikaans that I feel to some extent describes where I fitted in: *laat lammetjie*. It means something along the lines of 'the little lamb, born late'. This phrase expresses how it felt for me, being the youngest in my family, but it doesn't convey the deeper consequences of being what, in English, is called 'the runt'. I always felt I was somehow in the way, a nuisance. To compensate for this inner sense of rejection, I adopted the role of family mascot, always looking on the bright side of life and forever ready with a joke.

Mum had been warned not to have a third child, or it could very possibly kill one or both of us, but despite this Mum fell pregnant with me. I believe she developed a coping mechanism for her fears about the impending birth/deaths, by cutting off her feelings about my tiny existence. Guidance and counselling were not an option in those days; people simply had to use what they had. Her culture and era was one of poverty, suppression and denial, which translated into rejection as far as I, the unborn, was concerned.

Right from the start, my life felt like a fight for acceptance. I had no means of figuring out that I was not responsible for the feelings of other people. It was never explained to me that Mum did the best she could with thinking of himself as Cassius Clay. He would stretch my nerves and frustrations to their limit by shadow-boxing, using me as his punch-bag. His fist would always stop short of my nose, but he drove me to a state of internal rage as he bobbed, weaved and ridiculed me. I never learned how to release my frustrations in an appropriate manner and everything just got bottled up. A hug from him would have been like water in a desert, but in our era, that was simply not the done thing.

So when the nun began her attack that day, she had no idea what she was stirring or how primed I was for a volatile reaction. She fell silent and went deathly pale when all my frustrations exploded and I snatched the pencil from her hand and snapped it in half right in front of her face. Through gritted teeth and tear-filled eyes I quietly growled, 'Just piss off!' – and I turned and ran out of the classroom. I was nine years of age, but I know in my heart that if that lady had tried to stop me, I would have physically attacked her.

Jesus thrown into the trash can

In my heart I felt that I had just told one of 'God's secretaries' to piss off. The enormity of my transgression started to hit me as I ran from that classroom, so much so that I stopped on the stairs in disbelief at my stupidity. I sat for a moment with my head in my hands, until my true feelings rose from within me. It was right there and then on those stairs that I took a good long look at this God of mine. I looked at this impersonal God who was sending my friends to hell because they went to the wrong school. I looked at his 'secretaries' who, in my perception, were nothing more than intolerant thugs and unfeeling bullies, and in my heart I vowed, 'Well, if

Chapter 1

Trapped by an Imaginary Reputation

There is a phrase in Afrikaans that I feel to some extent describes where I fitted in: *laat lammetjie*. It means something along the lines of 'the little lamb, born late'. This phrase expresses how it felt for me, being the youngest in my family, but it doesn't convey the deeper consequences of being what, in English, is called 'the runt'. I always felt I was somehow in the way, a nuisance. To compensate for this inner sense of rejection, I adopted the role of family mascot, always looking on the bright side of life and forever ready with a joke.

Mum had been warned not to have a third child, or it could very possibly kill one or both of us, but despite this Mum fell pregnant with me. I believe she developed a coping mechanism for her fears about the impending birth/deaths, by cutting off her feelings about my tiny existence. Guidance and counselling were not an option in those days; people simply had to use what they had. Her culture and era was one of poverty, suppression and denial, which translated into rejection as far as I, the unborn, was concerned.

Right from the start, my life felt like a fight for acceptance. I had no means of figuring out that I was not responsible for the feelings of other people. It was never explained to me that Mum did the best she could with what she had or that I was not the cause of any emotional coldness on her part. I was therefore never able to develop or nurture internal emotional boundaries that would in turn allow me a sense of individuality. I had no ability to protect myself from taking on the irrational and damaging feelings of others. Consequently, if ever there was a bad mood in the home, I would feel responsible, not only for causing it but for repairing it too. I had no way of setting limits around myself.

Primary school

I went to a Catholic primary school and my belief was that Catholics went to heaven and Protestants to hell. This confused me, but there was a sense of security in the thought of being on God's side. Most of my friends attended Protestant schools and I used to force out of my mind the idea that because they were not Catholic they would go to hell when they died. I never doubted this belief, because it was God's way and not to be questioned. Nuns, whom I found very intimidating, ran our school. I actually believed that these women were God's secretaries, in direct contact with him each night. They seemed to glide around school when we all had to walk. I had a twisted fear about these nuns, but I regularly cheated under their noses by copying during lessons, despite my belief that they knew everything. The fear of capture was there, but not the fear of consequences.

On one occasion during my first year at primary school, at the age of 5, I repeatedly asked for permission to visit the toilet, but was refused. I was having a genuine bowel emergency, but was just told, 'Hold it in until the class ends.' I subsequently failed to hold anything in, and I made one huge mess of myself! I desperately hoped that no one would notice. However, the class-room slowly filled with my smell, and people started laughing and talking about me.

Something in me died that day.

I received no help, compassion or apology. The teacher ushered me out of her classroom to be cleaned up. I became the butt of everyone's jokes because of the mess I made. I felt a traumatic amount of shame and an electrifying sense of rejection as everyone laughed at me.

All the other children abandoned me, and I had no means of freeing myself from what was developing into a destructive emotional state. I internalized all my hurt and shame, and very soon I was having graphic anger fantasies about anyone who, in my eyes, rejected me. Those fantasies eventually started to manifest them-selves in the shape of me picking on people. My self-confidence was very low, and the weaker people around me unfortunately bore the brunt of my simmering and potentially explosive turmoil. I felt a deep hatred for my teachers for causing me this torment, and I had absol-utely no respect for them.

A few years later I failed to answer any questions in a mathematics test. I simply had no way of working out how to answer the questions before me, and I therefore abandoned the whole exam. I hit a mental block every time I tried because none of the numbers made sense. So I was kept behind after school for 'private tuition'. The nun trying to teach me long multiplication on one par-ticular day totally lost her cool and struck me on the head with the point of her pencil several times, asking, 'Why can't you get this into your thick head?'

She hit a nerve – I blew a fuse!

In the home, although we had lots of fun, I was con-stantly up against the adversity of two older siblings. The in-house rivalry usually involved my brother Alan thinking of himself as Cassius Clay. He would stretch my nerves and frustrations to their limit by shadow-boxing, using me as his punch-bag. His fist would always stop short of my nose, but he drove me to a state of internal rage as he bobbed, weaved and ridiculed me. I never learned how to release my frustrations in an appropriate manner and everything just got bottled up. A hug from him would have been like water in a desert, but in our era, that was simply not the done thing.

So when the nun began her attack that day, she had no idea what she was stirring or how primed I was for a volatile reaction. She fell silent and went deathly pale when all my frustrations exploded and I snatched the pencil from her hand and snapped it in half right in front of her face. Through gritted teeth and tear-filled eyes I quietly growled, 'Just piss off!' – and I turned and ran out of the classroom. I was nine years of age, but I know in my heart that if that lady had tried to stop me, I would have physically attacked her.

Jesus thrown into the trash can

In my heart I felt that I had just told one of 'God's secretaries' to piss off. The enormity of my transgression started to hit me as I ran from that classroom, so much so that I stopped on the stairs in disbelief at my stupidity. I sat for a moment with my head in my hands, until my true feelings rose from within me. It was right there and then on those stairs that I took a good long look at this God of mine. I looked at this impersonal God who was sending my friends to hell because they went to the wrong school. I looked at his 'secretaries' who, in my perception, were nothing more than intolerant thugs and unfeeling bullies, and in my heart I vowed, 'Well, if she belongs to you, you can piss off as well! I don't want to know!' I threw my under-developed belief in God and Jesus into the trash can where it belonged, and in my heart I ran out of the school system.

After that, I started playing truant and forging letters of excuse 'from my parents' to the school about my absenteeism. In our culture and context, my parents were in fact better than most. Dad was a disciplinarian, yet quite approachable, with an amazing sense of humour. He rarely held back from displaying his love for Mum and all his children. He called her 'Blossom', and it just suited her. Mum was small, kind and, as far as I was concerned, easy to control, and yet I always felt like I was in her way.

Alan was the eldest son, with Linda in the middle and me the youngest. Alan came across as aloof in my eyes. I idolized him, but he was very much an individual. He set his sights on what he wanted to do in life and went for it. Alan was studious and stable. Linda was a little less studious. I had difficulty concentrating on anything – I was academically challenged and as insecure as they come. I always felt very protective towards Linda, but she was a girl in every sense of the word, and I was the little brother always in the way. We had many a fight between us, but we were taught never to go to sleep without making friends and bidding each other 'good night'.

My role models outside the home were late-sixties trendsetter types. Mods and Rockers were the rival gangs in England at that time, and our district, which was known as China Town, was predominantly Mod. The Mods would often gather on our streets on their scooters and ride off in twos, looking fantastic to us younger, 'wanna-be' Mods. Marco, the local Mod leader, unknowingly turned out to have a huge impact on my life. He had long hair, a scooter full of mirrors, a loud and carefree attitude, and one hand covered in tattoos. When it came to 'The Man', Marco was it, and this was the character type I secretly emulated.

My brother Alan was certainly an idol for me, but not in the same way as Marco. Alan was focused, funny, good looking, and in my eyes a wonderfully talented footballer. It was easier for me to emulate Marco, though, because he was a rebel and a drop-out. Alan was going to do well, and that threatened me. I was convinced Alan would play for Manchester United one day – so much so that I actually wrote to Sir Matt Busby, inviting him to watch Alan play in our local Sunday league.

Our home was a Manchester United home, and for every home game we would pile into my Dad's work van and shoot off to Old Trafford. For the first few years my friend Carl and I would get right behind the goal at the Scoreboard End to watch the likes of George Best and Denis Law. I would often imagine myself at the opposite end, known as the Stretford End, where, in my Dad's opinion, 'all the idiots went'. That was where all the very loud singing came from, including some very abusive songs towards the opposition. I always felt a pull towards the Stretford End and wanted to be in with the skinheads and boot-boys, as they were known.

I fantasized about being in among the thugs and trouble-makers. At an early age I started to see the police as an enemy. They were always getting abuse from the crowds, and I idolized those who went too far and were thrown out of the stadium by two or three police officers. My twisted allegiance to the thuggish element of the human race gave birth to an inner, unfounded dislike of the police. This resentment stretched even to hating the children of police officers. Near to where we lived was a newly built area called Park Drive. Several police houses were on this estate, and from time to time a crowd of us would run through this area looking for 'coppers' kids', and on finding any we would ensure they went home in tears. I grew to feel a deep stirring of contempt within me if a police officer simply entered a room or a bar that I might be in. In later years this was going to backfire on me.

I thought that I had many friends at the start of my teens because I lived in China Town, which was a very well-known district. However, unknown to me, the majority of my peers disliked me because I was always portraying myself as better than them. When our family moved from China Town in 1975 for the refurbishment of our area, on the eve of our leaving I was attacked by one of my 'friends' from behind and for no apparent reason. Three or four others surrounded me, ready to join in if I retaliated against the guy who had hit me. The punch on the jaw was nothing compared to the hurt of rejection from these guys. I went home with a lump in my throat because I was so disliked by the kids I'd grown up with, and resenting everything that my culture stood for.

We left 31 Branksome Road the next day in a furniture truck. I sat peeping out through the back doors of the truck as a chapter of my life closed with a deep sense of hurt and rejection. I believed the whole district was glad to see the back of me, but were too hypocritical to say it to my face. In my imagination I had expected a going-away party; in reality I got a smack in the mouth and a churning desire for revenge. I had rejected God, and rejection became my deepest enemy.

At our new home I soon experienced my first encounter with a chemically induced high. It came in the form of a bottle of cider shared with my best friend Langy. I did not start drinking heavily at that point, but the alcoholic virus had bitten me and went dormant within me. I remember a deep sense of release and relief as the alcohol took effect on me, and that would later become my motive for drinking and drugging when my emotional state became too much to handle. Drinking simply for pleasure was never an option.

My parents gave me permission to go to the United games with friends from school. We used to get to Old Trafford three or four hours early, in order to be at the front of the queue and so get a central position in the Stretford End. The two-hour train ride to the stadium from Stockport involved systematic destruction of the train, and hurling seats and lightbulbs out of the windows. From that time on, that was the story of my life – I was always right in the thick of it all. I would wear what I saw as my Man. United uniform: a red skullcap-type hat, red United baggies, a red sweatshirt and red Doc Marten boots. The trousers would be halfway up my leg and the boots polished. I was 15, trying to be 21. I was loud, abusive and, to all outward appearances, 'one of the boys'. But Mum and Dad made the rule that I should be in by 9 p.m. at the latest, and in bed by 10:30.

That year (1974) was a particularly bad one for United fans. At the end of that season, our 1st Division status was about to end; but even worse, Manchester City were involved! United needed Leicester to lose if we stood any chance of staying up, and on the last day of the season, our fate was in their hands – and they drew. United were relegated.

But the sting really came because United were playing City that same day. Denis Law, who had served and loved United for years, was now finishing his career playing for City, and it was actually Denis who scored, giving City a one–nil victory over us!

At the visitors' end the City fans were dancing with

glee. From the Stretford End there came a rumble for trouble. It went without saying that there was going to be a riot of some sort this day. I made my way down to the touchline, and got into a position where I could get on the pitch if anything happened. Normally, 15 minutes before the end of a match, the police would line up to prevent pitch invasions. So something like 17 minutes from the end, a couple of guys near me made a run for the pitch. Several police officers ran after them, leaving a gap for me – and away I went!

By the time I had run ten metres onto the pitch, United fans were pouring out of the Stretford End onto the pitch in their thousands. The players abandoned the match and ran for the dressing rooms. The police did an amazing job of keeping the two sets of fans apart, and the attentions of the stampeding fans went to the players' entrance, where we went to tell United we loved them regardless. A line of police officers linking arms secured the entrance.

At the last game of the season, every year since I'd been going, the fans went onto the pitch. It was an accepted tradition as a farewell until the next season. This time it was very intense because of the context, and in the atmosphere of aggression, I dug up a chunk of the pitch and threw it at the line of policemen. This lump of earth hit an officer's helmet, and only the chinstrap held it onto his head, by getting stuck under his nose.

Instantly I knew I was in trouble, and a deep sense of panic started to well up from the pit of my belly. I saw his face change to red with anger, and he fixed his gaze on me while straightening his helmet. I saw him release one of his arms from the chain, and I knew he was coming for me. I knew that I had no choice but to run.

As I turned to escape, I was blocked by something like 17,000 chanting United fans forming a sea of humanity.

The right arm of the law came up from behind me, under my chin, getting me in a headlock, hoisting me off the ground and off the pitch towards the players' tunnel. I suddenly became a 15-year-old schoolboy! I was babbling all kinds of apologies and excuses as this irate copper carried me away, simultaneously slapping me in the face with the palm of his free hand. He said something into my ear as he carried me off, but I only heard the menace in his tone. I kicked and struggled, trying to break free.

I said some very stupid things in those few moments of volcanic panic. I told him that my dad was an ex-paratrooper, that I was still at school, that I had asthma (a lie), that I was Catholic and wanted to be an altar boy (another lie). I really tried to reassure him that I'd never do anything like this again and that I'd learned my lesson. I said all that in what felt like the longest thirty seconds of my life. I saw from this that, lurking deep within me, at root level, there was a coward.

The coward within

Somewhere along the line I had heard of a 'custody room' at Old Trafford, where trouble-makers were taken and beaten up by the police. I had heard that the police would roll thugs up in a mattress, and kick and beat them but not bruise them. Because the copper was slapping me with palm of his hand, not wanting to bruise me, I therefore assumed that he was taking me to this custody room. I remember then seeing a door looming, and I really believed that this was the doorway to the worst beating of my young life. Somehow I managed to get one foot either side of the doorframe, and I went as stiff as a board, exerting every ounce of adrenalin-induced strength I could muster and yelling, 'You're not getting me in there!' over and over. I was writhing and twisting, tearfully growling, 'I am not going in that room!' It's amazing what absolute fear can do in a coward.

The police officer was fighting a losing battle with me, until a colleague of his got involved. My legs were removed from the doorframe and I was thrown into this room, still yelling. I was by now at a point of exhaustion and extreme tension, expecting a group of police 'hit-men' to attack me. Sweat was pouring out of me as I was thrown into what I believed to be a dungeon, feet first.

Once in, I was suddenly aware of a very pretty policewoman staring at me as if I had just fallen out of a spaceship. I then noticed a couple of secretaries and a very calm-looking police sergeant peeping over his spectacles at me. It was a charge office. I was so glad to see them! I stood there panting and sweating, my image in tatters and my reputation fast evaporating, and wanting to thank everyone for not being the hit squad.

When they started asking for my details I was more than happy to tell them everything. They asked me my name and what class I was in at school. When they asked my age I told them, plus what position I played in the school soccer team, and how Everton had once expressed an interest in me, but I was only interested in United. I was babbling with relief because I thought they were going to hurt me. Some skinhead boot-boy I was! I actually wanted to hug these guys for not wanting to beat me up.

It took something like two hours to process and charge me, by which time I was like a kitten in their hands. However, the instant they let me go, within three metres of the police station door, the 'thug' resurfaced and no one could have guessed the truth about who I really was.

I got home from the ground that night two hours later than normal. When confronted by my dad, I said I had been in Manchester with 'the guys', because I would not see them again until next season – and somehow he believed me. My terrifying ordeal of that day started to subside at last because my family were all around me. I looked at them in a new light that night.

News at Ten was on and just coming to the halfway point. It was my bedtime after the news. The close of part one always gave the headlines for part two, and on this night, the up-and-coming news item was 'Riot at Old Trafford'. I felt a surge of excitement that I had been involved in a 'riot'. I couldn't wait for school on Monday, and the stories I could tell – 'I was fighting with the police', 'I gave one of them a good hiding' – the possibilities were limitless! I was the man of the match that day, never mind Denis Law – in fact, 'I gave Denis Law a back-hander as the police dragged me past him.' Fame at last!

I was sitting on the arm of the settee. Alan and Linda were sitting on my right, with Mum sitting between Dad's legs off to their right. The television was just in front of me, to the left. We all waited for the news to come back on. When it did, I felt like my young life was about to come to an end. The trauma I had felt when that police officer broke ranks to come and get me, and the panic I had felt wrestling with him outside the room of death, suddenly felt like kids' stuff. As I sat there, still wearing my red skullcap, red sweatshirt, red baggies and red boots, on the screen in front of us, there was I, getting lifted off the pitch in a headlock by an irate bobby, and away up the players' tunnel!

There was a deafening silence. I could feel my dad looking at me, and my blood running down to my toes. The roof of my mouth suddenly held onto my tongue

and would not let go. I started to cringe inwardly and I
think one side of my face started to twitch. I felt as if I
was getting smaller and smaller as the news broadcast
continued to talk about 'arrests' and 'charges being
brought'. I became very aware of my skullcap, and my
boots, and that I really needed to pee.

Dad broke the silence by sending everyone but me
upstairs and turning the TV off. Even Mum was sent out
of the room and the last thing I heard her say, with a real
seriousness, was, 'Don't hit him, Fred.' As the door
closed behind my mum, I stared at it for what felt like a
lifetime. Dad simply sat staring at me. All I could do was
sit there on the brink of an emotional explosion and
wait.

Then it came. What struck me more than his words
was the shaking head of disapproval. During the tirade
of rebuke from my dad, I remember thinking, 'Can't you
just belt me and have done?' He went on and on at me:
'You lied to me, you looked me in the eye and you lied
to me, and to your mum! We believed you. You lied to
us!' I was sobbing as he expressed his hurt over how I
had lied to him. This big tough boot-boy caught a
glimpse of his true colours twice that day. Once when
the bobby was doing his thing on me, and then again
when my dad was giving me the roasting of my young
life. I was a fake thug, full of bravado.

However, the following Monday at school, I was once
again 'the man'. I believed the younger kids at school
were looking at me in much the same way as I had
always looked at Marco. In my mind, I became some sort
of folk-hero to these guys. I sensed they were looking up
to me in some way, but felt that if they had seen the real
me – wanting to give information not even asked for to
the police, and the sobbing wreck trying to apologize to
his daddy – they would have had a different opinion of

me. I was silently confused, but said nothing to put the record straight. I realized that I was trapped behind a reputation – a reputation enhanced ten-fold by my own imagination. Life turned inside out for me. When no one was looking, I would cry when watching *The Waltons*, yet I thought nothing of inflicting quite vicious assaults on people.

I started tattooing myself. You have to understand how strict a disciplinarian our dad was to fully grasp how insane the idea of tattooing myself at that age was. Dad never once raised a hand to hit any of us. He never had to. Right up to the day he died in March 2002, what Dad said, went. Frail and dying in a hospital bed and barely able to talk, he was unable to sit up, so he said to Alan, 'Help me up.' Alan very sensibly said, 'Just lay still, Dad' – yet he almost jumped to attention when Dad barked at him, 'Sit me up!' Alan obeyed. Dad just carried authority in his voice – he said what he meant and meant what he said. So if he said it was Tuesday, believe me, it was Tuesday!

I first of all tattooed a solitary 'gang dot' on my leg. It was easily hidden, and I inwardly enjoyed having this secret from everyone in our home. Next, I made a tattoo on my other leg – it was meant to be the symbol from *The Saint*, a very popular TV programme at that time. It should have been a matchstick man with a halo above his head. Because of my artistic inadequacy, it came out as an odd-footed devil, holding a fork twice the size of itself! It looked like a very childish drawing. I was left with a deeply embarrassing tattoo, and I hoped that no one would ask me what it was supposed to be. I had no concept of it being there for life. I never saw past the moment.

Determined to press on, I asked Marco if he would tattoo 'Col' on my right arm, and he agreed. Just as he started, Marco's cousin said, 'Have you any idea what his dad will say if he finds out you did that?' With that, Marco abandoned the tattoo half done. I was left with a very tidy 'C', not quite central of my right forearm. I told myself I could finish it, not for one moment considering the recent disaster on my leg, which had been done with my good hand. I now proceeded to try to finish the tattoo myself with my left hand, because no one was willing to put himself in my dad's firing line. I ended up with 'COL', and it looked like a child's writing.

I found the secrecy of hiding my tattoos at home a source of excitement to begin with. What became very typical of me, though, was the more I got away with, the further I would push something. Eventually I tattooed 'MUFC', in bold capital letters, across the back of my left hand, and my attitude had slid to that of 'stuff the consequences'. Such is the phenomenon of 'reputation'. Pretty soon I had the whole of the back of my left hand covered in tattoos.

All of a sudden, I become aware of people looking at me, in much the same way as they looked at Marco. I thought it was with some sort of respect; now I see that for the most part, they regarded me with confusion, contempt and sometimes even pity. From time to time I would catch a glimpse of myself in a mirror or a shop window, and I would think, 'What the hell have you done to yourself?'

My reputation actually ruined any opportunity there may have been for me to make it as a professional footballer. This sounds like boasting, but I honestly think I could have made it with any of the big clubs of my day. However, having a 'reputation' prevents one from being natural. The true self gets suppressed, and even your talents become negatively infested. We are not created for oppression or suppression, because it causes a false and damaged personality.

By the time I was considered by professional talent scouts, I was emotionally trapped by what I thought I had to be. My reputation did not allow me to lose in the game I truly loved. Defeat, for me, was always personal, and it stirred up horrible desires for revenge. I was actually afraid of this venomous passion to win that was within me.

When the scout from Everton Football Club asked to watch me play, with a view to inviting me along for trials, it proved too much for me to handle. I felt I had to be the invincible one, supposedly afraid of no one, and known for rioting on television. Now, however, there was the possibility of someone seeing through me, and telling me I was a fraud, or not good enough.

I simply told them I wasn't interested. I *was* interested, but I was afraid of making a fool of myself. It was as if the real Colin, the naturally talented footballer, was slowly drifting further and further out to sea on a piece of driftwood, and no one could hear his cries for help and understanding.

I was also offered trials for Stockport Boys, but my parents could not afford new boots for me, and I had to go in a tatty old pair. All the other kids had sparkling new kit, whereas I had a hole in the seat of my shorts and two pairs of school socks on because my boots were two sizes too big. The shame was immense.

My reputation worsened when I got into a fight at the trial and was asked to leave. I remember being totally fed up with being poor. I was 14 and my hopes of soccer stardom had been dashed.

Cider and cigarettes didn't actually give me a good feeling, but they did seem to take away the bad feeling that I carried around within myself all the time. So from the age of 14, I was drinking for the effect. I didn't like the smell and the taste of alcohol, but the feeling of 'drunk' was far more preferable than anything 'sober' had to offer me.

The Mods of that era had hit the local headlines more than once for things like gang fights and drug possession. The thought of drug possession appealed to me far more than the gang fights. I loved the terminology used by the older guys around me, like 'getting busted for drugs' and 'over-dosing on smack'. I entertained this new language in my mind, and pictured myself 'getting busted'.

I was heavily tattooed, I was smoking and drinking, and I threw my virginity away, all for the sake of my reputation. My mum and dad had actually instilled in me a healthy regard for the one-man-one-woman picture of marriage. Dad often boasted about not even kissing Mum until they were engaged, and even then only on the cheek. He treated Mum like a rose, and actually called her 'Blossom'.

My virginity went up in a cloud of cider and smoke two years before I left school. I remember actually being disappointed in myself for throwing this virtue away, but that truth also got suppressed along with everything else. The act of sex itself was a huge let-down. I was clumsy and selfish, and regularly noticed that my partner, Tina, was disappointed in my performance.

I felt a deep sense of dread and intimidation as my schooling was coming to an end, and it was time for exams. I did absolutely no revision for any subject. With a reputation to maintain, I couldn't stay in and study. While an atmosphere of seriousness descended over most of my school peers, I ridiculed the whole system and showed them all my middle finger. I failed everything they put in front of me.

I was more interested in becoming what William White, in his book *Pathways*, calls a 'pseudo-junkie':

'Pseudo junkies are individuals who, for whatever reason, have been unable to find any social niche in life, but who have discovered a certain identity and acceptance within the culture of addiction that is more satisfying than their life experiences offer.' Although I had not yet interacted with the culture of addiction for long enough to establish an identity, a dissatisfaction with normality had set in, so it was more of a probability than a possibility that I would become part of that culture.

I was already fluent with the gift of persuasion, so I managed to get a decent job after leaving school, just for the sake of appearances and expectations. I talked my way into an apprenticeship in mechanical engineering, specializing in automatic gearboxes. With the weekly pay-packet, though, came the opportunity to fulfil my increasing desire to get into the drug scene. I started to flirt with amphetamines, and I suddenly discovered that they met my every need. They gave me a sense of euphoria, they took away my appetite and they also took away the need to go to the toilet! They made me brave, friendly and funny. I actually felt as if people liked me – so much so that I talked to them whether they wanted me to or not. My hair had grown very long, and my attitude was loud and carefree.

Yet inwardly I felt that something was drastically wrong about my life. My inner pain had been anaesthetized, but it had not been removed. I just stopped feeling it. But when the effects of the drugs started to fade, so too did my desire and ability to relate to people as their equal. I started to feel a deep sense of insignificance. My thought-life through the working week revolved around the last and the next weekend's amphetamines. They became my motivating influence. They gave me a greater sense of identity than I was getting from my girlfriend Tina. They gave me a sense of power, of knowing everything – a sense of invincibility. These feelings generated my desire for drugs. On the other hand, withdrawal always felt like it was going to last forever, and it brought on a sense of fear, shame and guilt.

I was 17, and already sliding downhill. At home it was Mum, Dad and myself. Alan and Linda were married by this time. My job called for me to revisit the classroom once a week at college. Nothing had changed. The lecturer may just as well have been talking French as far as I was concerned when he waffled on about percentages and ratios and the internal combustion four-stroke engine. I was soon falling behind in my studies once again. The sketches I had to draw as part of my studies were like those of a four-year-old. I was deeply ashamed of my child-like efforts. I was internally screwed up because of my inadequacies and my seeming inability to absorb and learn, because I also knew that I was by no means daft. What bothered me most was that it appeared to me that everyone else was confident and getting on with it. I felt like I was the only one struggling.

Losing control

I inwardly sensed that I was taking drugs too often, smoking too much and drinking too much. I also realized that I was really quite lonely inside. It was at this time that I went through some really heavy rejection from my first love, Tina. She wanted to have a baby with me, but with all my other confusions, I could not agree to it.

We never made love. We simply got drunk and had sex. I had no concept of lovemaking wherein both

parties reach sexual fulfilment. It was all about my satisfaction. This relationship felt like it was made in heaven
to me – I thought we were made for each other. Tina,
however, felt differently. The novelty of going out with
me wore off for her and reality destroyed her fantasy.
Over the two-year period of the relationship I had the
attitude that I was doing her a favour. Tina eventually
started to grow up though, and inevitably she dumped
me for someone else.

I was deeply heartbroken by this. Tina and I had
found our 'first love' in each other and our daydreams
had always been of a future together. I was totally devastated that it all suddenly meant nothing to her. I went
into a stage of not washing, even after a day working in
a garage. Oil was ingrained into my skin and hair and I
just didn't care. I went through the motions of work and
college, but I was preoccupied by thoughts about Tina
and this guy, and what I would like to do to them for
hurting me. My mum was very ill at this time, but I was
too wrapped up in my own teenage world to fully
appreciate the extent of her illness.

Then one day, at the peak of what I thought was the
worst of emotional storms, and just when it felt like it
could not get any worse for me, Dad, Alan and Linda
arrived at college in our car. I somehow instantly knew
that my mum was going to die that day. She had suf-
fered from cancer for eighteen months, and that day she
died whilst I sat holding her hands. She simply faded
away.

As I watched her final breath leave her, I stopped feeling. I did not feel angry or confused or even sad. I did
not feel any more pain about Tina and her new
boyfriend. I simply did not feel anything. I emotionally
switched off. As the week progressed, though, and with
everyone around me crying, the enormity of it all began

to sink in, but I covered my feelings with a 'brave face'. I did a lot of care-taking in those first few Mum-less weeks, making sure everyone else was all right and displaying a false courage.

The only feelings I had were of a self-pitying nature. My thoughts would regularly drift back to Tina, and how I could maybe win her back by means of pity. I hated my thought-life and the fact that I did not feel like everyone else looked. I felt no loss, no remorse and shed no tears. As I tried to bluff my way through my grief about Mum, denying the hurt of losing Tina, I then heard that she was pregnant from her new boyfriend. They say when it rains, it pours.

My teenage heart got harder and harder as I went into the eye of this emotional hurricane. I did not wash for the week leading up to Mum's funeral. My hair was long and very greasy, and on funeral day as I stood at the graveside, looking into this hole containing a box with my mum in it, I felt nothing. I was aware of family and friends around me, with many of them weeping, and yet in truth I was actually wondering what they were thinking of me in my untidy state.

I remember one thought, as clear as if it was this morning. It was simply this: 'If I'm not careful now, my life will totally fall apart.' I could not focus on my mum dying for any longer than a second or two. I could see it all at an intellectual level, but as soon as any corresponding feelings began to stir, I ran off in my mind, and invariably ended up in thoughts of a self-centred nature.

I went to work the day after Mum died and then the following week I went college. There was a side of me that actually enjoyed the fact that I would now be at the centre of attention with a justified sympathy story.

The lecturer at college asked me, 'What happened to you last week?'

I said, 'My mum died.'

Then he said, 'Oh, I'm sorry. I know how you feel.'

I inwardly exploded with rage. I just got up, walked out of college, went to work and resigned. As I walked away from college, the world around me felt totally empty, worthless and meaningless. I didn't want anything from anyone. Life meant nothing and carried no direction.

'I know how you feel' was the worst thing anyone could have said to me at that point. I was in personal turmoil because of my academic disability and the inner sense of impending failure. I knew at an intellectual level that my drinking and drugging was getting out of hand but I could do nothing to stop it. I had been dumped by Tina, and to top it all off, my mum had died practically in my arms. No one knew how I felt. Even I didn't know how I felt.

I spent the next nine months or so just bumming around, sinking lower and lower into my own well of self-pity and loss, not knowing how to release my inner turmoil. And then, just when I thought things could not possibly get any worse, my home life started to disintegrate. I started to fall out with my dad. He was drinking every night, and sobbing in my lap about my mum. At first I used his grief to avoid my own. If I could be there for my dad, then I would achieve some sense of purpose. Unfortunately, though, I heard the same stories night after night, and I actually began to hate him. I dreaded him coming in at night because the crying would start. I was frozen in my emotions. All I could feel was anger towards these alcohol-inspired weeping sessions.

I did use them to my advantage, though – I would coldly dip into his pockets whilst he wept, or I would emotionally manipulate him in his vulnerability to get some money for my next day's drink and drugs. I was injecting amphetamines by this stage (1975–6). Nothing else really mattered to me by this point. I simply got a false high as often as I could, yet inwardly knowing that it was all falling apart around me.

Then one day I went to a hairdresser in Manchester and instructed him to shave my head. The guy was stunned into silence. My hair was very long and naturally curly. He said people would pay to have hair like mine – and here was I, having it all shaved off! I had seen something, though, and made a decision. I joined the British Army that afternoon.

Earlier I had walked past an Army Careers Information Office, and seen a guy in uniform on a poster in the window. This soldier was young, healthy and good-looking – all the things I was missing. I remember thinking, 'That's how I should feel,' and yet I had to concede that I was not involved in relationship with anyone around me. I felt totally alone in life and isolated from anything warm or healthy. The only relationship I was involved in was with the chemicals that I put into my bloodstream. I had to take the initiative.

I left Stockport within two months. I saw a glimmer of joy in my dad's eyes as he and Linda saw me off on the train. I couldn't see anything of Linda's eyes, because she was sobbing like a lunatic at her baby brother going off to war. I was only going to Aldershot!

It kind of went without saying that I would join the Parachute Regiment, because that was Dad's regiment. However, I sat and watched a film about the different regiments, and when I saw the Parachute Regiment, with these guys falling out of an aircraft, I had one thought: 'Balls to that!' I joined the Transport Regiment, hoping to get a Heavy Goods Licence. The trucks were big and looked a bit intimidating, but at least I would not have to jump out of them from 2,000 feet! Dad sounded disappointed when I told him over the phone that I had not joined his beloved 'Paras'. But this was me taking the initiative, and I remember thinking, 'You'll have to get over it. I'm doing this for me!'

Chapter 2

Military Service

I was accepted into the Royal Corps of Transport and became 24457602 Driver Garnett, C. It was a fantastic adventure, meeting up with guys of the same age (18) who were also embarking on the same journey. Friendships were formed instantly and were of a quality quite unique to the military. However, within two weeks of joining 65 Training Regiment RCT, I was in serious trouble and in line for a Court Martial.

The first set of lectures we got on our induction was about 'Team Building'. The continual message was, 'The guys around you are your buddies; with them you fight and die, if need be.' It was all about teamwork and sticking together. It worked. Our first weekend out on the town saw fourteen of us drinking in Aldershot, all trying to drink an impression on the other. At the end of the night, a fight broke out, and a guy to whom I had grown particularly close, Ecky Mitchell from Scotland, was being held up against a fence and punched mercilessly by a guy twice his size. I was about 50 metres away and all I heard was, 'The Paras have got Ecky!' I took off towards the fight and was running flat out by the time I got to the scene. As I arrived, the guy who had been doing all the punching was just getting up off the floor. I didn't break my stride, and kicked him across the side of his head, instantly knocking him out. I knew I had gone too far, and that I may well have killed the guy.

Everybody stopped when this happened and I disappeared into the town. I later walked back and past all the police cars and two ambulances. The guy I had kicked was being loaded into an ambulance, still unconscious and bleeding from his mouth, nose and eyes. I knew it was serious. By the time I got to the back gate of our camp, the police were at the front gate. I managed to sneak in the back door of my billet, just as the Military Police were storming the front door.

I shot up two flights of stairs and just dived into my bed, turned to the wall and pretended to be sleeping. The boots coming down the corridor were studded and very loud. It sounded as if there was a battalion of them, and they were all coming my way for some reason. My room's door opened, and four or five really heavy-duty Military Police officers came right up to my bed. I just lay there, hoping beyond hope that they would go away.

An eternity passed, and one of them placed the brass tip of his pace-stick under the blanket near my chin and, with one flick of the wrist, he hurled my bedding to the other side of the room. The three other guys with whom I shared the room were all in exactly the same condition – deathly silent, too scared to move, hoping it was all a dream. It wasn't a dream. With my cover removed, I lay there wearing a red sweatshirt, blue baggy jeans and red Doc Marten boots. There was the sound of their boots backing away from my bed, and then one of them uttered an ear-piercing bark: 'On your feet!'

I jumped up onto my bed and tried to scale the wall behind me with the palms of my hands and the soles of my boots. I was in sheer and utter panic. The sight of a high-ranking officer had a twofold effect on me. Initially I was relieved that a beating was out of the question, but then I realized that I was going to face a very serious charge.

They said nothing more and simply marched me off to the Military Police Station. I was stood to attention in a little room near a charge desk at 11:55 p.m. – I could see a clock through the open doorway. A lot of action was taking place just around the corner from where I stood trembling, but no one said a word to me.

After approximately an hour, a Military Police corporal came and stood right in front of me and said, 'The lance-corporal you kicked has lost his eye, and with it his career with the Parachute Regiment.'

I was left alone again, and nothing further was said to me. At 4:45 a.m. I leaned forward to ask if I could use the toilet, and the corporal came and shouted right in my face:

'Who said you could move?! You will stand stock still until you are instructed to move, and if you move before then you will be beasted¹ beyond anything you could ever imagine! Because if you think you can blind a military man and get away with it, you are sadly mistaken! And when we get you to prison we will have our fun on you, boy, before we send you home in disgrace! And if you pee on this floor you will clean it up with your tongue! Is everything I just said understood?!'

The 'Yes, Corporal,' seemed to come from someone else. Nothing made sense to me; I thought to myself, 'Was that me?' I write this thirty years after the event, but that Military Policeman's verbal onslaught remains forever etched on my memory. I can still almost feel his breath on my face and see his fillings.

I spent the rest of that weekend in close custody. I was put in a cell and told that whenever anyone entered my cell, I had to be stood to attention by the time he got there, and before he asked me anything, I had to tell him, at the top of my voice:

'24457602 Driver Garnett, charged under section 33a of the Army Act 1955 and sentenced to close custody by the commanding officer of 65 Training Regiment Royal Corps of Transport. I have no requests or complaints, Sir.'

They tell you this once, and by some strange phenomenon, you remember it. A bit like remembering that Military Policeman's response to my toilet request!

On the Monday morning I was marched before the colonel. He read the charge to himself, looking up at me several times as he did so, before sitting back and breathing a long, deep sigh. I had two escorts stood right in front of me, burning their eyes into me and breathing on me.

The colonel asked me, 'What happened?'

As calm as you like, I simply said, 'Sir, I've been here two weeks. All I have heard since I got here is "Stick by your buddies through thick or thin; never leave your buddy." Well, Sir, that's what happened. My friend was getting beaten up. I put a stop to it the only way I knew how.'

From that moment, I became a hero. I went from zero to hero in one statement. They kept me in custody because civilian police were involved, but the Regimental Police Staff were now giving me cigarettes and even the odd can of beer as I became the flavour of the month. I was soon allowed back into regular training whilst on bail for Wounding with Intent to Cause Grievous Bodily Harm, awaiting trial at Winchester Crown Court.

Because the incident took place in the town, the civilian police decided to prosecute me. This was not good. It probably meant a prison sentence and dishonourable discharge back into civilian life. For the moment, though, I was 'the man' to be around, and I suddenly found that I was once again developing a reputation. A reputation for being tough is not the wisest thing to have in the Army, because there really are some truly tough guys in there, but even they seemed to respect me.

By the time the court case came up, the Army were well pleased with my progress and were going to defend me as best they could. The guy I had kicked, as it turned out, was suspended from duty at the time of the fight for bullying new recruits. I made a plea of guilty at the Crown Court and the Army representative sang my praises for the best part of twenty minutes. I walked out of court with the only punishment possible for me to keep my uniform – a fine.

Germany

Within a few months of the court case I was shipped across to Germany. I slotted right in when I arrived in Germany because it was a drinking culture, with mad-cap behaviour being the norm. My time in Germany was spent mostly on camp. Every time I went in town, I got into trouble. I started becoming known by different regiments, and with that came an inevitability that I would soon have to fight their top guys. I was inwardly extremely fearful about this. My nerves were shattered by it all. I hated the drink, but it gave me a false sense of calm. I failed to see that the intake of alcohol was at the root of all the trouble, and that the withdrawal from the alcohol was at the root of all the fear I felt on a daily basis. I did two years in Germany before going to Belfast for a six-month tour of duty there. I was 19 going on 20, and inwardly very insecure in that volatile atmosphere.

Alcohol was supposedly rationed. We were allowed a maximum of two cans per night. Most of us, however, somehow managed to down twelve or fourteen cans each night. While the majority of the Regiment sat chatting in a respectable manner during time off, I would be in the thick of a crowd who were falling around drunk and stripping off on tables, singing football songs and smashing the place up. Whilst drunk on New Year's Eve, I rang home to pass on seasonal greetings, and Linda had a cry down the phone because 'her baby brother was at war'. I decided I was going to stow away on a ship to Liverpool and make it home by lunchtime the next day. I simply started to walk out of our camp in the very centre of Belfast at 11:30 p.m. The guard at the gate came out to stop me staggering out into the city, and I pulled my Browning 45mm on him and walked him backwards to the wall with the barrel under his chin. I woke up on my bed the next morning, with a momma-sized headache, and several aches and pains all over my body. To this day I don't know where they came from, but I do know that I got the kicking I deserved and they saved my life.

I was on the Bomb Disposal Team, having been chosen from 300 men to train to drive and operate a seventeen-ton armoured water-cannon. This vehicle had never been used before; I was the first British driver to operate it. The incident on New Year's Eve cost me this position. I was up before the colonel again the next day, and he gave me a choice: I either accepted his punishment or I was transferred off the team. I opted for transfer, claiming that I blew it and would need a new start somewhere else.

What no one knew was that I used to lie awake in the early hours of the mornings in a state of extreme stress about the size of the job before me. Everyone around me held me in high regard on the team. I was a very important cog in a mind-blowing system, but it always felt like they were seeing something that was not there. I thought they were being fooled by my reputation. It simply went without saying that I was dependable in a crisis, because of my introduction to the service and my madcap attitude in daily life.

But the truth was, I was very intimidated by it all and would have relished the chance of voicing my insecurities to someone, but that was unheard of. Had I been given the right counselling, I believe I could have been dependable in a crisis, but the backlog of years of suppressed, frustrated fear and shame ruined my stability and I was always in a state of inner anxiety. I lived in fear of a life-threatening crisis, believing I would blow it at the moment of truth, never connecting my irrational fears to the amounts of alcohol from which I was withdrawing.

What I failed to see was that, at crisis point, I actually did do OK. During a vehicle breakdown recovery on the outskirt of an IRA stronghold called the Ardoyne area, I was assigned point watch, meaning I was to cover our front. I was standing in the back of an open-topped Landrover with my rifle, scanning the houses and streets in front of us, when I noticed a car with two guys in the front very slowly drive past our operation. I caught the eye of the passenger and we almost respectfully acknowledged each other.

It crossed my mind that they were impressed by the size of the operation. We were hooking up two fifteen-ton military vehicles, with troops scattered in various positions for cover. I saw the guy smile at me and he looked me straight in the eye. Their car kept moving very slowly. Approximately 150 yards away, they stopped. Smiley got out of the passenger seat, crouched down next to a streetlamp and brought a pistol up to the aiming position. It was him and me.

My drill should have been to yell something really silly like 'Gunman dead ahead!' to my comrades, and then a warning of 'Halt! Hands up! I am ready to fire!' to my smiling friend. Instead, I very calmly decided that he could have the first shot with his pistol from 150 yards, and then I was going to kill him and then blow the back of the driver's head off as he drove away.

I got the guy dead centre in my sights and waited. I even anticipated how long it would be before he fired, and I adjusted my breathing to prepare for sending him a 7.62mm bullet. No panic – just the right amount of fear, and a smidgen of pleasure, and I knew that this guy was mine.

God bless him, though – he bottled out. He must have known the futility of his exercise, because he suddenly jumped into the car, and away they sped.

On our return to Germany the whole Regiment hit the town. We had done a tour of Belfast with only one casualty – a guy lost an eye when some sort of missile hit him. The feeling was good. On my way back to camp on that first night back, I leapt from a speeding taxi in an attempt to avoid paying, as one does. I tore almost every ligament and tendon in my ankle and lower leg. My right leg was blue and completely swollen.

I eventually woke up, in several inches of snow, just inside our camp gate, and right opposite the Guard Room. It took me a few minutes to work out that I was looking at it from the outside, and then the pain started to seep through the now fast-fading alcohol. Somehow I managed to crawl the kilometre or so to my billet, and slip into bed. Less than twenty minutes later, I was being carried to the medical officer. He had no choice but to launch an enquiry. I went up before the colonel again, on crutches this time, for questioning.

I kept saying, 'I don't know, Sir.'

He thought I was protecting someone and soon got fed up with me. He said to me, 'Well, this blows your month of home leave; soldiers are not allowed to go on leave on crutches – it wouldn't look good.'

I placed my crutches against the wall in his office, and told him, 'With respect, Sir, I'm going on leave,' and I managed to very slowly walk out of his office without limping. The pain very nearly caused me to pass out.

I was given back my crutches and I made my way across the ice-covered parade ground, concentrating on not falling. I felt terribly afraid and lonely in the middle of that parade ground that morning. I started to sense that my superiors were getting fed up with me. I went home for a month's leave.

I could not find a girlfriend at this time of my life because I was always in some sort of fracas. I was extremely lonely. I would lie on my bed most nights and look with envy at guys who had pictures of girlfriends by their beds. I had never really known intimacy. Actually I was deeply afraid of it, because of the pain it usually brought. Love songs would come on the radio and I would imagine myself singing them to an imaginary girlfriend.

On my return to Germany, I soon got into a fight on camp with a guy who punched me from the side without warning or apparent reason. These things often seemed to happen to me. I so infuriated the people around me. The two of us decided to go behind closed doors and punch it out. I battered him for ten or fifteen minutes before getting arrested by the Regimental Police.

There I was again, up before the colonel for fighting. Colonel McDonald offered me an alternative to prison. He said I could fight him. I chose prison. I was given twenty-eight days of detention, which included extreme beasting and daily humiliations around camp. The rest of the regiment went on manoeuvres in Canada whilst I was serving that sentence, and at my release interview I asked the colonel to return me to England, because I felt like I had let everyone down and I needed a fresh start at a new regiment. I was on a plane within a week. I left 'C Troop of 4 Div RCT' without saying goodbye to the guys, and that was the most painful part. I left in shame, with my tail between my legs.

I was transferred to Marchwood Military Port Support Squadron and placed in a small troop of men responsible for the UK's in-land movement of stores and ammunition. This simply meant we were trucking all over the UK, having a laugh.

Military prison

The military still held me in high regard and offered me every opportunity to resurrect my fast-fading career. I was even appointed Colonels' driver to an international shooting competition to be held in Aldershot. I was back where the fun had started, but with an opportunity of somehow making amends this time. I was on my best behaviour, until my first night off. I went for a drink in the same town centre. I drank alone for three hours. On my way home, I ran into a packed taxi rank, kicking and punching at three guys who had said something to me as I had staggered by. I ended up getting chased back to camp before being arrested by the Military Police again. I was sent back to my regiment in shame. I was given another prison sentence for assault and bringing my squadron into disrepute. During these terms of detention, I would actually shine as a soldier. I was too fit for them to break in the gym, and I was always clean and smart.

I had met a girl from Manchester around this time and I ploughed all my emotions into this woman. It felt like

I had been starved of love, and so I almost devoured her. I rang her every night from the Detention Office and served my sentence without her knowing about it. She had no idea of the kind of idiot she was involved with; she just thought she had met a soldier.

There was one particular sergeant major who everyone hated and feared, and who hated everyone but feared no one. He was the ugliest thing I had ever seen. He was a prisoner's nightmare. No matter what your cell was like for inspections, he would come in and destroy it for his own pleasure.

The same song had to be sung every time he or any officer walked into my cell: '24457602 Driver Garnett, charged under section 33a of the Army Act 1955, sentenced to 21 days' detention by the Commanding Officer of 53 Port Support Squadron, Royal Corps of Transport. I have no requests and no complaints, Sir.'

Every time this guy was on duty he did two things. He would throw my kit all over the cell, and he would verbally abuse my regiment. The throwing of the kit did nothing to bother me, but the remarks about my regiment really got to me. He came into my cell towards the end of my sentence, and knowing exactly where I was going, I sang the song for him, but this time with a difference: '24457602 Driver Garnett, charged under section 33a of the Army Act 1955, sentenced to 21 days' detention by the commanding officer of 53 Port Support Squadron, Royal Corps of Transport. I have no requests but one complaint, Sir.'

The silence was deafening. The whole guard staff sat up to listen. No one had ever complained, especially to this guy. One simply did not complain. He walked right up to me and got his nose touching my nose and he said, 'What is your problem?'

I was stood to attention, looking straight ahead. I had learned never to actually make eye-to-eye contact with an officer, but to simply stare into space somewhere in the area of their forehead. To voice my complaint, I shifted my eyes down ever so slightly in order to look him directly in the eyes. I then smiled and quietly said to him, 'Sir, in my opinion, you are an arsehole.' No one else heard me but God and him. I was past worrying about either.

He went ballistic. He was gesturing me to fight him in my cell, calling me all the names his filthy vocabulary contained. I simply stood there. At one point I looked at him and started smiling at him – this was like throwing petrol on a fire. He was going crazy. But I knew two things: he should not have been in my cell on his own, and he was not allowed to slander my regiment. Every other officer would have a regimental police officer with him. But this guy came in alone each time he came.

When the duty regimental police officer made his report out about my complaint, he could only quote the sergeant major, and even then it was all abuse and threats. Up in front of the colonel, I lied through my teeth, in the midst of the truth about him criticizing my regiment. I made him look like the instigator, supported by the police report. Once again I went from zero to regimental hero.

Following that sentence, I was appointed driver to the Royal Marines. These guys were unbelievably smart and switched on. They were, in my opinion, The Best. So to be appointed their driver was a real honour and a pleasure. They were stationed in Portland and doing manoeuvres from a ship berthed down there. My job was to drive them wherever they requested. I slept on board their ship, and I just enjoyed watching the *crème de la crème* of the British military at work.

One night we had a late-hours drinking session, Marines versus Army. We were all out to impress one another. Once again, I drank like a pig, but somehow managed to find my bunk. Just before it got light the next morning, I woke up on the brink of peeing. I had no time to waste with things like looking for the loo. I shot up the nearest stairs and just about made it to the side of the ship. There I stood, in my shorts, like a fountain-head, urinating over the side of the ship. I got goose-pimples from the sense of relief, and I started to relax and to break wind, as one does. Never satisfied with half a job, I cleared my nasal passages and spat over the side too.

Then it came – the dawn of a nightmare. I fell into a pit of internal horror as I turned to go back below decks. The Royal Marines were on parade, stood stock-still, in their best uniform, being inspected by their top brass! My life flashed before my eyes. I actually tiptoed back to the stairs, hoping they had not seen or heard me.

I was once again sent back to my regiment in shame. As 1980 arrived, my military service was coming to an end, and I could not wait to get away. My Regimental Sergeant Major called me into his office and took his beret and belt off. This meant it was all off the record from here on in. He asked me to sit down, and he asked me to seriously consider what he was about to tell me.

He said, 'Colin, you are not cut out for civilian life. You are a squaddy through and through. If you get out in June, it could prove to be the worst mistake of your life. If you extend your service for another six years, I will send you home for a month and then send you any-where in the world for six months, with a guarantee of promotion when you come back.'

I sat there speechless – not so much about the sugges-tion, but because of the genuine concern in this hard man's voice. And he called me Colin! I just said, 'Sir, I'll sign.'

We filled in the forms together, still on first-name terms of Colin and Sir, and we reached the point where all I had to do was sign my name. I picked all the forms up and said, 'I need to phone my girlfriend.' He sat back, shaking his head, and threw his hands in the air.

In the phone booth, I tore the forms up when I heard my girlfriend crying. I left that phone booth, telling myself that I had not made a mistake by telling Julie. I refused to believe that all she truly thought about was herself and not what was best for me.

I went back to the sergeant major's office. By this time he had his whole uniform on and when I told him of my decision, he called me a rude name and dismissed me.

By the end of June 1980, I was back in Stockport, where I immediately started to see that nothing had changed. In every pub I went in, it dawned on me that the same people were sitting in the same seats talking about the same superficial things and repeating the same jokes to each other, as they had over three years before. I had managed to reach a Class One standard of driving, so I was never out of work for long, but the sergeant major had been right – civilian life is for civilians.

I had experienced things like marching in a body of men to a military band. I had experienced the painful struggles of doing basic training with a team of friends, and the victorious pride of completing it. I had tasted the sweetness of a passing-out parade where our training was recognized by family and ranks alike. I had seen the tears of pride in the eyes of my dad. I had gone through hell and high water with guys just like myself. I had seen active service on the bomb disposal team in Belfast. I had jumped out of aircraft over Germany on a free-fall course. I had had a whole catalogue of wonderful experiences with the Army and made amazing friends.

I had in fact become the young soldier I had seen in the Army Careers Information Office window three years earlier, and more – but I still felt inwardly dissatisfied and angry. What the average civilian saw as entertaining, I now thought to be utterly boring and dangerously superficial. What the average civilian saw as friendship, I saw as fickle and unhealthy.

My drinking soon became extreme, as did my violence. Julie and I decided we would get married. I promised her that I would go the romantic route and ask her father's blessing on our marriage. I had to build up the courage to ask him for over two weeks. I knew he was not at all impressed with me.

The first two words I spoke to him, in his own home, had been a very aggressive 'Shove off!' I had been drunk and sound asleep in his house before he arrived home, and he shook me to wake me up. I didn't know where I was or what the shaking was about. Apparently I sat up, wide eyed, looked him straight in the eye and growled my obscenity at him. He staggered backwards and I slid back into the chair to my slumber.

I didn't quite make it back to sleep, though. The silence was deafening. I was in that no-man's-land somewhere between sleep and waking, and I started to wake up. I was thinking, dreading, that that had been Julie's dad at the end of my verbal trash. I was just starting to hope that I had dreamed it when I heard his voice in the background: 'I won't be talked to like that in my own home!' I knew I was in trouble. I stirred and tried to pretend I had no idea what had happened, but the damage was done.

So when the time came, I nervously approached the subject of Julie and me getting married, and he started to shake his head before I even got the question out. He simply said, 'No.'

I shrugged and thought, 'Screw you, mister – I was only trying to be polite! Who needs your say so?'

He went on to say that 'Julie will never marry.' He was right.

After long persuasion from Julie's mum, he agreed. Julie and I got engaged and a party was thrown. I got ridiculously drunk, and wondered why everyone else was being so reserved. I treated it like a NAAFI session and was staggering around drunk, being very rude to everyone I met, making it plain that no one enjoyed my sense of humour more than I.

Chapter 3

The Relief of Prison

Dad had met another woman by this time, and when I walked in one night and saw her for the first time, I knew there was going to be trouble. She was a drinking buddy for my dad. She was sprawled out on the floor with her skirt undone and a bottle of vodka next to her.

I looked at my dad and simply said, 'Get this fat cow out of my life!' They broke up quite soon afterwards, and Dad went back to coming in drunk and sobbing in my lap about Mum. I was right back to where I had been when I had joined up.

In the end I took hold of him and yelled at him, 'Dad, shut up! She's dead, man! Stop digging her up every night!' It visibly shocked him, but I knew he was unable to break free from his torment.

By 1982 I was drinking too heavily, smoking too much weed, back on amphetamines and having the occasional flirt with heroin. I was gradually promoting myself from the status of 'pseudo-junkie' to that of 'working-class junkie'. As a 'working-class junkie', one simply creates relationships with other 'workers' revolving around drugs and their usage. Each day is a struggle. A good day is defined by the quantity and quality of the drugs the worker has managed to find and use.

Active addiction

By the start of 1983 I was injecting two or three times a day.
I was stealing from my dad, my girlfriend, her parents, her
sister and my employers. I lost my driving licence and my
job in 1983. Julie then made a decision to get pregnant
before ending our relationship, telling me never to come
near her or the baby. I visited her in the hospital when I
found out that she had had a boy, and as soon as I walked
into the ward I knew she did not want me there. I asked
her if my suspicions were right. She said they were, asking
me to leave. I stared at her for a few moments. She had
changed. She had what she wanted – now there was no
more need of me. I was inwardly devastated.

I simply went out and picked up a single mother of
three, called Sue, in the town's seediest nightclub. I started to sleep over at Sue's house at weekends, using it as
a break from my dad's nightly bouts of sobbing.
Nothing had changed in me. It was all about my gratifi-
cation when it came to sex.

Soon I was also visiting her mid-week. I started to go
out from her house in the middle of the night with
another heroin user, Alex, and we would commit burglaries throughout the night. We never came back
empty-handed. By the end of 1982 I was committing a
burglary a day to fund my heroin addiction. I wanted to
stay off the drugs, but it was quite simply impossible.
One or two days without drugs would cause an emotional storm in me. I experienced extreme anxiety that I
just did not know how to handle. I took the drugs to stop
myself feeling bad. To buy the drugs, I had to do things
that I hated and made me feel bad, and for that I needed
more drugs. Life was a swamp of pain and frustration.

I did, however, find one area of comfort – Sue's children. Joseph was 2, Matthew was 4 and Sherane was 7. I

found that I could just be myself with them, and once the initial worries about 'this new man' were out of the way, I felt very safe with them. I felt very protective about them and wanted to father them. We had tensions, but there never seemed to be any resentment that lasted between us. Joseph (Jo-Jo) called me 'Dad', and I loved it. Matthew tried to call me 'Dad', but he had experienced quite a lot of his real Dad, and so it was a half-hearted attempt. Sherane saw me as Colin, and that was really nice.

I arrived at Sue's one afternoon to find her crying in the kitchen. She looked at me and said, 'I'm pregnant.' I thought it was the best news ever. I made all the right noises about never leaving her, and giving up drugs, and settling down and so on. I then went out and injected heroin to celebrate. I then decided to move in full-time with Sue and the children.

By the time the baby was born in December 1984, I was serving my first civilian prison sentence for ten burglaries. During the build-up to that sentence I became fifteen kilograms under-weight and went into a severe spiral of physical, emotional and spiritual deterioration. My family members often looked at me with shock, and from their reaction to me I would see the true extent of my decay.

Inwardly I longed to go to prison because I felt like I had to, in order to belong in the tribe I was running with at that time. Everyone had done time but me. Finally, I got my wish. The psychological and physical withdrawal I experienced in prison was like nothing else on earth. I went without sleep for seventeen days and sixteen nights – not one minute's sleep! For the first two weeks I went through a physical nightmare of sweats and backache, but the sleeplessness was a killer. I was doing two sentences: days and nights.

On the seventeenth day I lay down after my lunch, as was the norm, and all of a sudden I was waking up. I could hardly believe that I had slept. I started sleeping from that point, getting a little bit more each passing night. It was two months before I was getting a full night's sleep. Mr brother Alan came to visit me at the start of that sentence in Manchester, and as he looked across the visiting table at me, I could see that he was going to start crying over what he saw. Everything within me wanted to say, 'Please don't cry! What will people think of me if they see you crying?' I was totally self-absorbed.

Hayley

I met my daughter Hayley for the first time over a prison visiting table, and the simple sight of her stirred all my innermost desires and longings for normality. And yet prison actually offered me a sense of relief from the frightening and counterfeit relationships of civilian life. I was heroin-free only by incarceration, but my promises and determination to stay off heroin when I got out were very real to me. My letters to Sue began to fill with plans of staying drug free when I got out and getting a job and settling down. Within the darkness of my soul there were now glimmers of hope. Hayley was my reason to live now – she gave me a purpose in life that I'd never had before. I wrote all this in letters to each of my family. I was now drug-free and going to the prison gym five times a week. I felt strength and determination. I truly believed that I would stay clean now. Hayley was the final piece to my picture and the source of my motivation.

I came out of prison in March 1985. Within three days of release, I was back to using heroin and amphetamine by needle. It seemed to hit me like a runaway train. All I wanted was simply to have £5 worth of heroin, 'just the once'. I just wanted to sort of say good-bye, have one more for old times' sake, one for the road kind of thing – and before I knew it, I just got totally swept away by it all.

I stole the clothes Sue had bought to look nice for my homecoming and I sold them for less than a third of their value. I stole a gold chain from around her neck – she thought I was just being affectionate, tickling her neck. I was very quickly back to robbing a house a day and spending anything up to £250 a day on heroin and amphetamines.

I had truly believed that the prison sentence and Hayley's arrival had changed me. I deeply believed that my love for her was strong enough to keep me clean. I then started to believe that getting my driving licence back would change me. I convinced everyone around me that this was true: 'I'm at a loss without my driving licence. Once I can work, it will all work out.'

Then eventually I got my licence back and found work. I soon discovered that work actually got in the way of using drugs. I reasoned that I should be able to work and, by what I earned, govern the amount of drugs I used. Every morning though, fearful of going into the day without a hit, I would drain diesel from the truck I was driving and sell it for £25. I would then park the truck on the side of the road, mix the heroin with vinegar and water in a spoon, burn it for ten seconds or so and then inject it. The smell of the mix caused severe retching, but nothing was going to stop me having this hit. Once I had injected, I would aim the vehicle in the general direction of wherever it was I was going, and somehow get on with a day's work. I also took amphetamines during this period, but heroin was my first love.

Inevitably my employers would eventually work out that the diesel was not going as far as it should, and I would be confronted. On more than one occasion I simply shrugged and said, 'I've been selling it to buy drugs,' and I would then walk off. Every firm I worked for, I robbed in this way. My desire for heroin and amphetamines really was insatiable. I was never satisfied. I actually started wanting to go back to prison.

On one driving job, where the company were very keen on diesel receipts, I stopped the truck in the middle of the afternoon in a busy, built-up area. I could see from the truck's cabin that a house was empty of occupants. I got out of the truck and walked up the garden path. On my way, I picked up an ornamental rock from the garden and, without concern about there being anyone in, I simply hurled the rock through the front window. I sliced my wrist on the glass and blood pumped out of me, but I had seen a video recorder, and it had £150 worth of heroin and amphetamines written on it, so I carried on with blood going everywhere, and I stole it.

During another raid on a house, I noticed something about myself, but I could not tell how long it had been happening. I got back into the truck and realized I was having to fight to stop myself from crying. I was thoroughly sick of it and hated every minute of this life I was trapped in, but I could see no other way. I often saw deep sadness in my family's eyes every time I met with them, but the madness continued.

I was in and out of court for drunk and disorderly behaviour and criminal damage and things like that. Sitting in the waiting rooms of the Magistrates' Court at Stockport on one of these silly charges, I saw a lady tap in the code on a digital door lock and then enter an office. I saw that she had pressed one number from the top and two from the bottom. When she came out of the office, I walked up to the door, pressed what I thought she had pressed, and unlocked the door. Once inside, I ransacked all the drawers in the office, looking for drug money for after my case was dealt with.

Then I heard the combination lock being tapped and I dived behind the door. Another woman walked in, but she didn't see me behind the door. I pushed her to the end of the office and ran for it, down two flights of stairs, past several startled police officers and court officials. They knew something was wrong, but no one tried to stop me. As I got to the bottom of the stairs, I heard the woman screaming, 'Stop him! Stop him!' Too late – I was out into the town and gone.

The headlines of the next day's *Manchester Evening News* read: 'THIEF BRINGS COURT TO STANDSTILL'. I sat staring at the headline with an inner sense of celebration – so much so that I told everyone in the pub that it was me who 'froze the system'.

Then exactly one year later, in the same courtrooms at Stockport, whilst waiting to be called up for criminal damage, I noticed a solicitor hanging his long, trendy overcoat in the changing rooms next to the interview room. I walked through the interview room, put the overcoat on, checked myself out in the mirror, and walked out wearing it. The headlines in the *Manchester Evening News* the next day once again read: 'THIEF BRINGS COURT TO STANDSTILL'. This was how my life was at that time – flitting from one opportunist crime to another, just about getting enough money to buy some heroin for that day.

I was soon back in prison, and my letters to Sue sounded just like the ones I had written during the previous sentence: 'I am off the heroin and amphetamines, and I can see that it was the drugs that were destroying me.' I wrote pretty much the same to all my family:

'I have learned my lesson now, I have a daughter, and a woman who loves me. I can get work and I really do not want heroin again.' I was very aware of the repetition, but I actually believed everything I was saying. Every letter I wrote, and every promise I made, I believed. I would lie awake at night and inwardly celebrate the fact that I was off the powders.

I still felt ripped off by Tina, who had given birth to my son – and even more so now because I kept hearing from second-hand sources that he had some problems with his growth. I also secretly longed to contact Tina for reasons of unresolved hurt. But all these frustrations were denied because I had a little girl to whom I could direct all my love. Hayley had brown eyes like my mum and I, and no one knew the joy that this little girl gave me. I was going to be her all-in-all as soon as I could sort myself out.

Overdose

I went back to prison for ten burglaries. Once again my letters were full of remorse: 'This time, when I get out, I'm not going anywhere near the stuff.' I was very convincing, because I actually believed it. I never told a lie in all my confessed failures and expressions of hope.

This time I saw Hayley once a month and had to settle for watching her run around a prison visiting room, and my resolve to get it right for this little lady grew stronger by the week. I convinced the parole boards and probation officers of my sincere determination to go straight this time. My family were once again sucked in by my ability to talk the talk, and Sue and I once again looked forward to a future free from drug addiction.

I got out on parole on 22 December 1986. All my promises to stay off heroin stood strong for two days. On Christmas Eve afternoon, I woke up in intensive care wired to a heart monitor, surrounded by several medical people, with a drip in my arm and my hand. I had overdosed injecting a drug that had been stolen from a chemist the previous night. An old friend of mine, Gary Ball, had actually kept me alive by heart massage and by injecting my lifeless body with cocaine each time he revived me, until the ambulance arrived.

I had gone to the pub on Christmas Eve and had a couple of bottles. I then heard about the chemist being robbed. A sneaky suspicion told me that if anyone would know who had stung the chemist, Gary would. When I got to his place, he had somehow got his hands on a lot of the stolen drugs. I assured him I had not had any booze, and we shared a hit of Palfium in his kitchen. My lights went out.

My twisted logic had told me that I could have a couple of these pills and get away with it, because they would not affect me like heroin did. I woke up wired to a heart monitor, with a 'peep, peep' sound echoing into my soul. I somehow knew that the sound was that of my life on its approach to flat-lining. In panic I sat up and removed the drips myself and fought my way out of the hospital. I somehow managed to get home and into bed before Sue had heard anything.

This incident scared me. I lay in bed with what I believed to be a blood clot on my brain – so intense was my headache. My head was pounding for hours. When I felt strong enough to stand up, I went into Hayley's room and took my sleeping daughter in my arms, watching her chest rise and fall with her precious life breath, and wondered why the hell I was willing to flirt with death without consideration for anything or anyone. Hayley was the one bright spot in a terribly sad and lonely life. During the darkness of my prison sentences, I always managed to get a picture of her next to my pillow. This picture became my sustenance in the darkness. I would smoke a weed or take powders and pills with other prisoners, and then at night I would silently touch her face and inwardly vow to get clean for her.

I worked pretty much the whole of 1987. The overdose really scared me, but as the year passed, I started to believe that I could stay clean now. That belief then grew into a very destructive message in my mind: 'I could actually have a hit of heroin from time to time.' So on Christmas Eve, exactly twelve months on from my last overdosing, I went to the house of a guy whom I knew had some white heroin. I convinced him to give me a hit. He put a little bit of heroin in a spoon in his kitchen, and I laughed at him. I said, 'Kevin, don't insult me – put some more in!'

I woke up again in intensive care wired to a very similar-sounding heart monitor, surrounded by very similar-looking medical staff, with a drip in my arm and my hand. It was like an eruption of panic. I sat up and tried to remove the drips myself once again, but this time I became very groggy and a nurse had to quickly remove them for me, because I was starting to want a fight with them. I clearly remember her saying, 'Oh, another smart-alec,' and I instantly thought of the previous year's episode – she was referring to that. I sat with my head in my hands after my escape, with a terrible sense that life was never going to change.

By April 1988, I was back inside for a burglary where I had had a confrontation with an occupant in the middle of the night. I had entered his house without noise, but got over-confident as I removed furniture and fittings to sell the next day. Gary Fitzpatrick and I were scheduled to visit Gary's life-long friend Johnny Hester the next day in Lancaster Prison. John was a good friend to both of us, but Fitz and John went back years. I did this burglary with the thought of, 'I'll get the small TV, and whatever I get for it, I will buy a drug parcel for John.'

As I was leaving the house with the TV on my shoulder, the owner was standing at the bottom of the stairs, and he nervously asked me what I was doing. I picked up on his fear and capitalized on it. I said, 'I'm robbing you. Go back to bed!' He hesitated for a second, until I walked towards him threateningly, and he gave in to my intimidation and turned and went back upstairs. He had already phoned the police, though, and before I could hide the TV, the street was surrounded.

I tried to hide in a garden, and once again I found I was crying, feeling a really deep sense of sadness. My feelings were overwhelming. I felt a deep sense of shame about how the guy had just had his domain raided by me and had actually had his self-esteem broken into a thousand pieces by my heartless behaviour. All the insanity was back in full glory.

I lay under some very uncomfortable bushes, in the dark, staring into nowhere, with tears on my cheeks. I saw a policeman peering over the fence into the garden where I was hiding. I saw that he had seen me, and I then heard him calling for the dog-handler. I knew that he was going to send the dogs in, but all I could think about was the state of my life. A dog attack did not worry me in the slightest.

The dog was let into the garden and soon found me, but for some strange reason didn't pay much attention to me. The officer was trying to excite the dog against me but it ignored him and explored the rest of the garden. I eventually stood up and held my hands where everyone could see them. I noticed people in nearby bedroom windows watching this middle-of-the-night police hunt, and I remember feeling jealous of their 'normality'.

I was eventually bundled into the back of a police van. A police officer whom I knew climbed into the van with me and said, 'Colin, what are you playing at?' I simply sat there and said, 'Mr Buxton, I need help.' He actually voiced disappointment in me, because he saw potential in me.

Deep inside of me, though, I was haunted by my failures and the damage I had caused within my family and society. I'd robbed my dad's house in recent months and he had very aggressively disowned me. I had tried the 'Poor me, everybody blames me' routine again, but it had lost all value. He had looked me right in the eye and had said with a heartbroken tremble, 'You are not the boy we gave birth to; I can no longer consider you to be my son,' and he had walked out and slammed the door behind him. That door echoed in my empty heart for years. He had washed his hands of me.

Sue had sat down trembling after Dad had left, and she had simply said, 'Oh, Colin.' She was in a deep state of despair over me. I had stormed out, robbed another house and bought heroin and amphetamines.

I looked at Mr Buxton and shrugged. I felt inwardly hopeless, and started looking forward to the jail and the gym. I made a guilty plea the next day and was remanded into custody. During the ride from Stockport Magistrates' Court to Strangeways Prison, I knew I had to go for rehab. Once I'd settled on remand I wrote to Sue once or twice just to tell her that I was going for rehabilitation after this sentence. I got no response. She and everyone else were in shock because of my rapid fall back into using, overdosing and crime.

It was at that time in Strangeways that I found the address of a Christian rehabilitation centre in the south of England. The idea of 'doing rehab' held an intriguing form of interest for me, just like going to prison had. I almost felt like I would have to 'do rehab' in order to reach higher levels of recognition within the addiction culture. But I must say that there was a deep desire for help too. I was sick of making promises I could not keep, and so I decided to just keep my mouth shut and do something about my problem.

Me going to jail was a relief for everyone, myself included. Some of the Christians I wrote to visited me in Strangeways and then invited me to go and stay with them. When I went to Crown Court, I put it to the judge that I needed help, and was going to rehab regardless of his decision – either instead of prison or after it. He decided that a prison sentence was unavoidable, due to my record, and I got fifteen months.

It was water off a duck's back. I was safe in jail. I always managed to get a smoke of weed for the night-times and I used the gym every day. I had three meals a day guaranteed and a bed to sleep in. Prison was not a problem. I did ten months out of the fifteen. I was deeply serious about cleaning up. Working the kitchen in HMP Risley gave me access to home-brew booze, but such was my seriousness about getting clean that I felt no attraction to the stuff. I wrote every week to the rehab, giving them details of my week and my dope usage. I was dead straight with them.

Fitzy was also locked up at this time and we inter-acted with inter-jail-mail through our sentences. I was due out six days before him and was forever reminding him that he had longer than me to go. That went on until I got a visit from Marco. He brought me a chunk of weed and the screw spotted him handing it to me. I got dragged off the visit for 'suspicion of smuggling drugs in Her Majesty's Prison'. I'd actually swallowed the chunk, so the charge stayed at 'suspicion'. I lost seven days, putting my release date a day after Fitz's. Needless to say, he revelled in this.

Fitz got out on the Thursday, I got out on the Friday, and that night we climbed the fence back into the prison he had come out of and dropped off four big bags of booze and drugs for the guys inside. For a brief moment, both Fitzy and I were on this incredible high. We had been released from jail, we had then broken into a jail and we were on heroin and amphetamines. We were the men of the moment, and we felt invincible, unmatchable, invisible and uncatchable. This was the desired state, but the price one has to pay is unbelievable.

My heart was breaking over my separation from Hayley and the fact that I was going to rehab, but I had to concede that my love for her was simply not enough to get me clean. The power of my addiction was stronger than the love I had for my child. This was confirmed to me when earlier that day, having just been released from prison, I went straight from the prison gate to Marco's house, and he gave me a bag of amphetamines. I injected the whole bag in two hits, and only then did I go to see Hayley, by which time my affections were actually false because of the speed. The best way that I can describe my state at this time is that I was in a state of 'high-depression'. The speed took me up, and the heroin satiated my downs, but the pain of loss and failure remained.

In 2004, Marco (Steven Markland), the Pied Piper of China Town, who everyone loved in their own way, died alone in his little flat from severe crack abuse and probably a deep sense of disappointment. By nature Marco was not a drug addict. He was a lovable rogue who made lots of money. He flirted with crack cocaine once or twice, and it swept him away like a tornado.

Let me share one more memory of Marco. As kids from China Town, we would regularly visit the fairground. On one particular visit, one of us got a clip around the ear from one of the fairground workers. We were aged between 8 and 12; Marco would have been 18 or 19. As soon as Marco heard that one of us had been hit, he changed into scruffs, and walked five miles or so to the fair to fight the fairground worker. As Marco strode out to the fair, he had something like thirty kids behind him. He was like the big brother everyone wanted. Needless to say, he kicked that man's backside!

In March 1989, less than a week after my release, I somehow managed to break away from Stockport and made my way to St Vincent's rehab in Andover. On my arrival at St Vincent's I felt a sense of relief because it was off the main road, and surrounded by trees. I spent seven months at the rehab, but in all honesty, it was just a hiding-place. I was training on weights six days a week, eating good food, and growing physically. I manipulated my way back into the life of the mother of my son from that rehab. I was writing to her and Sue, getting both of them to send me tobacco and money. However, when I suggested seeing my son, the door was once again slammed firmly in my face. I swallowed the resentment and the rejection once again. I just carried on as if everything was normal with Sue. Deep within me, though, there burned a desire for some sort of revenge for all this pain.

The rehab did not push the Christianity issue on us. I was allowed to go to the Catholic services. Everyone else went to a nearby 'happy-clappy' church. The guys used to try to get me to come with them, telling me that the music was excellent and the women were plentiful. I just declined and got on with the Catholic thing. These guys were Protestant and going to hell, or so I had been taught as a child.

Then one morning, the staff called us all together and told us that a guy called Billy Graham was visiting the UK, and was inviting St Vincent's to his crusade. I was not in the slightest bit interested, until they said, 'It's at Wembley Stadium.' I instantly knew what I was going to do. In a flash I said, 'I'll go.' I spoke to no one, but I had a plan.

On 8 July 1989 we all went on the same bus to Wembley, but no one knew that I had a tennis ball in my pocket. In my heart I vowed, 'I'm not missing this opportunity.' The St Vincent's guys all sat next to each other in the stadium, and for some weird reason we were in the Royal enclosure. I was sat ten or so seats in from the aisle. The songs of praise that were sung captivated me, but I felt very self-conscious about joining in. The stadium was filled with about 55,000 Christians.

Eventually this American guy came onto the stage and, in my opinion, waffled on for what seemed like an eternity. All I was interested in was trying to work out how to execute my plan.

Towards the end of Billy's sermon, a bolt of lightning exploded right behind him. All 55,000 people gasped, but Billy didn't blink. He just preached on. At the end there was an altar call for salvation. I sat on the edge of my seat. One of the St Vincent's staff looked at me, and I just stood up and said very convincingly, 'If I don't answer this call tonight, I might spend the rest of my life regretting it' – and with that I stood up to go forward.

Everyone stood to let me out, and I made my way to the pitch – the Hallowed Turf! I got more and more excited as I got closer to the pitch. Just as I got to the bottom of the steps, I looked back to see if the guys were watching me.

There was an eruption of excitement building up in me because of what I was about to do, and it had nothing at all to do with Billy Graham or the God he had waffled on about.

As I looked back, I was frozen in amazed horror to see everyone else from the rehab coming forward. I was deeply distressed, but I had made it this far – I wasn't going to back out now. As I reached the turf, I took my tennis ball out of my pocket and dropped it to the grass. It was then, on 8 July 1989, that I, Colin Garnett, proceeded to kick a ball on Wembley's sacred turf!

As I looked up, Alison, the woman who managed St Vincent's, was looking at me with deep disappointment in her eyes. I just shrugged. I didn't care. *I had kicked a ball at Wembley!*

Everything then suddenly went very quiet as Billy Graham prayed for people and led them in the salvation prayer. I picked my ball up, my heart pounding in my chest with adrenalin, and then bowed my head in prayer with everyone else. At that point, I repeated the sinner's prayer and sort of asked Jesus into my life. At the end of the service we were given a little booklet to take away and fill in every day. I threw mine away as soon as we got back to St Vincent's. I still refused to go to church with the happy-clappies, and just went back to my weight-training routine.

Three months later, in October 1989, after seven months of hiding, I walked out of the rehab. I was bored with hiding. I had developed for myself a comfortable situation out of an uncomfortable context. Within four hours of returning to Stockport, I was injecting amphetamine, smoking weed and drinking very heavily. I got arrested that very same day for possession of a stolen credit card. I was stopped in the street and searched, and ended up in the police cells by lunchtime. I was fingerprinted, charged and bailed within a matter of three hours. I was going to use the credit card to get kitted out, because I was much bigger physically than I had ever been. I had been eating very well and pumping iron six days out of every seven.

Some guy on my first night back insisted on being sarcastic with me, trying to pick a fight. I punched this guy with every ounce of anger within me, and the same feeling I'd had when I'd kicked the guy in Aldershot took over – I truly believed I had killed him. As I punched him, the bar we were in fell silent, and I then heard a lady behind me, utterly shocked, saying, 'Oh, good Jesus!' The guy fell and whacked his head on the pool-table on the way down. He was out like a light for ten minutes, with a split face which needed nineteen stitches. I had to flip him over onto his face because the blood was pouring into his mouth.

I started to feel like I was always going to be in the heart of trouble, and a sense of despair started to sprout within me. The next day I injected amphetamine.

This relapse actually took almost two years to gather momentum, and it was November 1991 before I got nicked again. I was trying to hold down a job, be a husband to a lady for whom I had no love, be a father for three children who were not mine, and be someone Hayley could look to for guidance, whilst keeping an amphetamine and heroin habit alive by committing at least one burglary a day.

I tried trucking again, and often found myself going off on a long-distance run which would take me away for three days. I would be sweating with withdrawals from heroin because I'd had none for twelve hours, so the prospect of going away for three days would haunt me. It eventually reached such a state of desperation that I parked the trailer of the truck on a nearby industrial estate, and went cruising the streets in the cab section in the middle of the afternoon. I noticed a lady leaving her house and locking the door behind her. Making my mind up that it must be empty, I gave her five minutes and set about the burglary. I was aching within my bones for a hit and saturated with sweat.

At the back of the house I found a spade and simply used it as a bat to smash the window in. It was 1 p.m. I heard the TV on in the front room but thought nothing of it, because people regularly left their TVs on for effect. I just walked in and went for the video under the TV. As I picked it up, a guy jumped out from behind the door and challenged me. I raised the video above my head and very quietly said, 'Sit down and shut up.' He sat down and I walked away with his video.

By the time I got to the truck, I was crying, sweating and bleeding from a head wound from the window. I got £75 worth of heroin for the video, injecting half of it at the drug dealer's house, and the other half just before I left the industrial area where the trailer was. I was then meant to go away for three days without drugs. I went back to the depot and resigned without excuse. The thought of leaving the drugs for three days was on a par with the dread of going to the hospital to see my mum die. I could not bring myself to leave the area where the powder was. Welcome to the life of a drug addict!

Cultural reject

At the start of 1991, whilst committing an afternoon burglary, I made a decision to press the palm of my hand against a window at my point of entry. My reasoning was, I had only been out of prison for a few months, and already I was right back where I had left off. At this rate,

I would need a 'jailbreak' by the end of the year. I needed and wanted to go back to jail.

On 7 November 1991, at about 5:30 a.m., several police officers burst into our home and arrested me for 'suspicion of burglary'. They gave the address of the house in question. I said, 'I did it.' I would have admitted to anything, but as it turned out, it was the house with the palm print.

It took them almost twelve months to trace that palm print to me, and I was right – I was in need of a break. I was actually relieved that I did not have to face another day of wondering where the next hit was going to come from. The mind works extremely fast at times, and on this particular morning, I heard the police coming through the front door, and I knew I could escape through the window if I chose to. However, I summed up my options, and had to concede that going to prison was my best option.

During the questioning one of the detectives asked me, 'What is an experienced burglar like you doing leaving palm prints?' I just shrugged, knowing that he would neither believe me nor understand.

The months prior to this had seen my graduation from 'Working-class Junkie' to 'Cultural Reject'. William White accurately describes these people as 'those addicts who, for a variety of reasons, are no longer in good standing with the culture. This category includes police informers, child molesters, or other addicts whose behaviour has become so outlandish that it poses a threat to the rest of the tribe.'

I had started robbing drug dealers' houses, violently taking drugs from some of them. I stole from Fitzy's flat, when the truth was that, in the midst of all this, he was the one guy who always had time for me. There was nothing sacred. Eventually one of the main suppliers blacklisted me and told all the other junkies that if they so much as spoke to me, he would blacklist them too. I was ignored by the ignorant and cast out by the outcasts. I became nocturnal, and many nights I would sit on a local railway embankment and cry about the loneliness and hopelessness of it all. All my intentions had once been healthy, but I could not fulfil them, and now I was resigned to unhealthy intentions.

So when the police barged in that morning, they were actually welcome. My solicitor came to me in the cells and shook his head about the prospect of me getting released on bail. I said, 'I don't want bail.' He just stared at me with a confused yet relieved look in his eye, and he then walked away. I was remanded to Strangeways yet again.

William White writes: 'Having lived outside society at large and having now been rejected by the culture of addiction, rejects become homeless and helpless, meandering in their isolation from institution to institution.' To me, jail was a relief.

It was November 1991, eight months after the riot in which prisoners had destroyed most of Strangeways. I'd spent somewhere in the region of three years in Strangeways, and the talk of a riot was always an undercurrent within the prison population. It was never a case of *if* – it was just a case of *when*. I had watched it on TV, from the loneliness of my own living-room, feeling envious of these guys pulling that place apart. I could very easily imagine the junkies raiding the dispensary, and then wanting sweets and tobacco; and the violence freaks wanting to attack the sex-offenders. I just knew there would be carnage in there, and inwardly wanted to be a part of it.

And now, here I was, back on remand, with no more than fifteen other guys, and prison staff who were being uncomfortably polite to us. We were given medication of our own choosing when that remand section of the jail first re-opened. I went for Diazepam, Temazepam and Valium, and spent each night sound asleep, and each day feeling as mellow as mellow can be. Life was really good.

I was, however, rapidly weaned off these drugs, and then I had a bit of a bad time of it. Once the withdrawals were over, I began to develop and come to terms with an inner fear of release. I was scared of getting out even before I had a sentence to speak of, and there was a corner of my mind that could see how sadly insane my state was. My family had washed their hands of me. Society's rejects had rejected me and I truly believed myself to be unemployable.

A ray of hope came in the strangest form. I got a letter from Sue, ending our relationship once and for all. She was not angry; she had just lost all hope of any reconciliation. I felt a sense of liberation, because that meant that it was now time to get real about myself, to myself. I also knew that it would mean severing all ties with Stockport for a period, and that would mean not writing any letters to or receiving any from anyone. I also had faith in my ability to manipulate Sue into writing to me and being there for me if I got out and had nowhere to go. I arrogantly believed that the relationship would only end when I was ready to end it.

Poetic expression

On H Wing, a remand wing of Strangeways, I was at a total loss for which way to turn for the future. Rehab had been a waste of time, and my record was worse now than last time, when 'prison was unavoidable'. But even more worrying for me was, 'What am I going to do when I get out?' Relieved to be arrested, no application for bail, and fear of release – I was in a terrible place. A headline in one of the daily papers leaped up at me in my cell one day. It said, 'BOY GEORGE, HEROIN ADDICTION'. I can very clearly remember thinking, 'Welcome to the club.' I did not bother reading it; I just brushed it off.

I was back in the gym each day, and this time I applied for education classes. It seemed that the attitude of the prison staff had changed and they just wanted a quiet life. I wanted to focus my mind on something. I was accepted onto classes and asked what I would like to do.

Without thought, I simply said, 'I'll have a go at poetry.'

The tutor pointed me towards a pen and paper and said, 'Tell me who you are in a poem.' I sort of got the impression he had said this once or twice before!

I sat down and, without a pause of any kind, I wrote this:

How It Is

The prison gives me 'thinking time', my life, my children, me.
To think of all the wrong I've done, and what I'd like to be.
To lie awake and ask myself: 'why lead this kind of life?'
Of using drugs, stealing things, no girlfriend, love or wife.
Throughout the day I scan the prison, a mission to find a sorter.[2]
That's not the way of a grown up man with a lovely son and daughter.
Life on the out was just the same, out stealing things for drugs.
Trying to be something I'm really not, with gangsters, thieves and thugs.

I've really got to sort things out or I'll just end up dead,
Another fool with an epitaph 'He never used his head'.
I've made our lives a misery underneath a huge black cloud
By forever doing what others did, by following the crowd.
But that was life behind a front, that's not the real me.
I'm Colin Garnett, I'm better than that, just you wait and see.
There'll come a time when once again I'll walk with head held
  high
But take nothing for granted friend, by the grace of God go I.
Because I lived fast on smack and speed, on morphine, dike and
  coke,
I showed my body no respect; life was just a joke.
I took the rides in the ambulances, woke up on the heart
  machines,
Filling my spike with too much drug for darkness, if you know
  what I mean.
So before you tell how bad life is, sit down and have a think
How truly precious life would seem if you were on the brink.
Believe me man, life ain't no joke, and neither is taking drugs.
You'll spend your life behind a front with gangsters, thieves
  and thugs.
Forget the buzz of making out; forget the sense of danger;
Just bear in mind your kids will grow to you a total stranger.

I called the tutor back and passed it to him. He thought I was being flippant, but as he read it, a smile began to crack on his face. He was smiling quite broadly by the time he finished, and he asked whether I had pre-planned it or had copied it from another source. I wasn't too put out, because I knew the truth. I actually enjoyed writing it, because it felt like I was expressing the truth about me, and for the very first time.

The tutor then threw a gauntlet down, with a patronizing tone: 'OK, then – write one for me about something we can all identify with – something from the recent news.'

I instantly knew what I was going to write about – the Strangeways Riot! What else? I sat down, took up the pen and within fifteen minutes had written this:

The Strangeways Riot

*As years passed by in Strangeways jail, tension grew and
grew;*
Inmates' protests got no response, so what else could they do?
The threat of grief was always there, but no one knew the truth;
Bad attitudes by all concerned cost Strangeways jail its roof.
*The nineties dawned, the summer came, and then the day of
fools?*
*The day the prisoners went to pray, with blades and wood for
tools.*
*The Chaplain Proctor blessed the men, 'The Lord God be with
you,'*
*Then a voice rang out 'now's the time' and they all knew what
to do.*
*The prison staff fled, they surely knew to fight would mean
defeat,*
So one by one they turned their tails and beat a swift retreat.
*Now the prisoners sensed a victory, and each man lost his
frown,*
For now the time had finally come to pull that prison down.
*The prisoners then fled from the Church; each one prepared to
fight*
Till silence fell and someone said, 'There's not a screw in sight.'
At this some felt disconsolate at loss of chance to feast,
*Then someone chuckled, 'Oh never mind, come on let's kill a
beast.'*[3]
*But many cons had other plans, and went for things they'd
seen,*
Like morphine in the pharmacy and sweets in the canteen.

Elation grew as the men were given the prison on a plate.
They stormed the landings, opening cells, releasing all their mates.
Now this blew up on April 1st, through ignorance and rules,
But who can say they did not know? The government? The fools!
The TV made the most of it, with radio and press,
They revel in all the misery, enjoying all the mess.
The public went to stand and gloat and watch that prison burn
And hustlers made the most of it as a chance for them to earn.[4]
Whilst in that jail some skulls got cracked and many minds got scars
By sights of paedophiles being slashed or kicked and beat with bars.
Upon the roof some thought it fun, stood waving to their mates
And picking police off hid below, bombarding them with slates.
For 4 long weeks those prisoners kept that prison under guard
With the police at bay, and the April sun, it wasn't very hard.
And now in Strangeways with changes made[5] *and attitudes improved.*
The cons can claim 'we made a point, we made the system move'.
But that's not to say, 'All is well' or 'happy ever after',
Because in that jail you'll often hear an evil wicked laughter.
That laughter comes in the dead of night and chills you to the core
And the cons just brood and wait, to wreck the place once more.

I hadn't noticed, but the teacher was watching me this time, and when I looked up, three or four other guys were watching too. My heart was pounding in my chest, and the power of what I was writing actually made me feel quite breathless. I sat back in a rush of adrenalin and started laughing. I wasn't in the least bit interested in what this guy or anyone else said or thought about my work. I knew it was mine and I knew it was brilliant. I was expressing myself; it was truth and it was liberating. Something very significant also struck home to me, but no one else mentioned it: God had made an appearance in both poems.

The tutor looked very seriously at me and said, 'Colin, did you really just write this?'

But he knew. Not only did he watch me write it, he saw my reaction to it, and that could not have been rehearsed. I heard him mumble the 'F' word, and he sat down as if he had just opened the winning lottery ticket.

I sold that poem to other prisoners for cannabis, and to prison staff for cigarettes.

The tutor challenged me to write something purely fictitious – something right out of the air. I went away to my cell and made my mind up to write it that night. But when I sat at my table and took up the pen, I drew a complete blank. Nothing would come at all. I threw the pen down after an hour or so in despair. This went on for three days and nights; it simply would not happen. I concluded that I couldn't write fiction, having now experienced the expression of truth. Then on 5 January, at 5:30 a.m., I woke up and, without getting out of bed, I reached for the pen and paper, and this is what came out:

From Prostitute to Nun

'Twas long ago on a star-filled night that the horseman came to town
Sat tall upon a horse's back beneath a silky gown.
His hair was golden, eyes were dark, beard trimmed and clean.
The town's folk knew without a word he was the strangest ever seen.

As children slept and the old folk dozed they knew that he was
      there
Because with this rider came to town a breath of clean fresh air.
Yet no one spoke or said a word; I think they probably knew
Who this man was and why he came and just what he would
      do.
The way he sat, so tall and proud, some said he had a glow
Of radiance and elegance, and his horse knew where to go!
Some old folk said as he rode by they felt a surge of youth.
Was this the one they'd waited for? Was this the man of truth?
So a silence fell but good will grew and they followed him into
      town
And each and every one of them sensed hope beneath that
      gown.
The procession grew and with it joy, some said a sense of love.
Was this the man they'd read about come down from up above?
The night chill seemed to fade away and a comfort came to all
But still the stranger sat aloft, still radiant and tall.
Now in this town there lived a whore who'd had her share of woe,
A bastard child born from a whore, the lowest of the low.
Some menfolk swore they'd never touched this child of ill
      repute
But all agreed she had lovely breasts and her smile was kind-a-
      cute.
The truth was though, she took her men at choice,
She simply had to purse her lips and use her sexy voice.
This night she sat up in her room alone and feeling down,
That was until the horseman came to the centre of the town.
That night her whole life brightened up, her heart filled up
      with pride.
The joy she felt she could not quell, the tears she could not hide.
For in her sleep a voice once said, 'One day a man will come
To put an end to your life of woe, he'll shine without the sun.'
With tear-filled eyes she looked at him and he looked back at
      her.

This was the man she'd waited for, of this the girl was sure.

At this point some men turned their heads to glance upon the whore.

They knew their 'fun' was over now, they'd use this girl no more.

Throughout the town there grew a fear stirred up by shame and guilt,

For each and every one of them had been beneath her quilt.

Now the horseman cast his eyes upon the menfolk of this town

But none of them could hold his gaze, in shame they all looked down.

Then from the heavens there came a flash, the town fell into prayer.

Then silence fell and then they saw the girl was sitting there.

Upon this horse the young girl sat with evil in her eye.

The menfolk feared the tide had turned, it was time for them to die.

The town wives begged, 'Please spare my man, please lady let him live!'

The whore just sat and laughed at them, 'You want me to forgive?

It's "lady" now my man has been, before my name was "whore".

You called me what you wanted to, but that's finished now, no more.

I've had your men, every one of them, they've begged between my thighs.

They came to me to satisfy their fantasies and lies.

But truth be known, I had my fun and adultery is a sin.

I've been the baddest of the bad by letting your men in.

So I'll forgive if you'll forgive and we'll get on with our lives,

And you can take your husbands home and be their loving wives.

But hear me now and hear me good, don't curse my name again,

> *Because the horseman gave me power you see, a power over*
>   *men.'*
> *They did not know that horseman said, 'Don't use this power*
>   *for wrong,*
> *Spread goodness girl, have faith in God and the power of*
>   *prayer and song.*
> *You've lived your life as a bastard child on shortages of*
>   *fun,*
> *But heartache leads to wisdom, child, so now become a nun.*
> *Go preach to men, plant seeds of love and try not to seduce,*
> *For a person's fate is determined by the tears that they*
>   *produce.'*

I walked up and down my cell that morning with my heart pounding in my chest. The excitement actually gave me a dull headache. I was totally amazed that something like that could come out of me – and once again, God had crept in. I was aware that God had been included in everything I had written, and it sort of spooked me. I felt that I had no right to use him in this way, but I also felt confusion because I had never intended to.

My court case date came through for mid February. Two weeks before my court case, Boy George was back on the front page of the paper, with a headline reading something like 'BOY GEORGE BACK ON TRACK', and there was an article about how he had spent two months in a certain clinic, and everything was hunky-dory for him again. I picked up my pen again and wrote to my doctor in Stockport. I simply said:

> What has Boy George got that I haven't? Is it because he is rich and I am poor that he can live and I have to die from this God-forsaken problem? What kind of country is this? United Kingdom, my backside! I come from as good a stock as he does.

Apparently my doctor sent that letter to a sister clinic of the one Boy George had been in, and they analysed it and offered me a bed with them for a fourteen-week therapy programme. Normal funding was £12,500 per month per person; I was being offered it for free.

In Manchester Crown Court, when the possibility of the clinic was suggested, all the court dignitaries considered my case, talking about me as if I was in another room, but all I did was set my eyes on the judge. Eventually she looked at me and I just spoke up. I looked her in the eye and said very politely: 'Your honour, prison is not working. It doesn't hurt. I need help now.'

Within two minutes she had made her decision. She said, 'I want to reserve your case to come before me in six months' time from this date. At that time, we will pass sentence for today's charge and you will be judged in accordance with the progress you make.'

Ten minutes later I was in my probation officer's car on my way to Clinic for Addictions in Lytham St Anne's, for what turned out to be one of the most significant periods of my life.

Chapter 4

Secular Therapy

The change from sharing a prison cell (where the toilet was open-plan, within a metre of the eating space) with a toothless and heavily tattooed heroin addict, to a thickly carpeted hotel-type room with a bell for room-service, plus a lawyer and en-suite facilities, sent me into a severe culture shock, to say the very least!

I was swept from one extreme end of the social scale to the other between a.m. and p.m., and was greeted at the door by several middle- and upper-class people wanting to hug me and carry my brown paper bag for me. People were saying things like, 'Hi, I'm Simon. I'm here for coke addiction,' and 'Hi, my name is Aveen and I'm an alcoholic.' I was shown into a huge rest room and offered a cup of tea. I think for the first time in years, I actually started to feel a sense of safety.

People kept telling me they were 30, 60 and 90 days clean or sober. Two guys sat with me and started to talk to me about 'willingness'. 'It depends on how willing you are,' they said.

My opening line was, 'If I'm told to drink gorilla snot in order to get clean, I will.' People were visibly shocked, but I meant it and felt no desire to apologize or impress.

I was a threefold mess: physical, spiritual and emotional. I could not deny the sad state of my heart any longer. My daughter was a forty-minute train ride away, and I knew no one could stop me if I opted for a runner. I also knew that if I allowed my love for my daughter to rule my choices, I would be dead by Christmas. I had to cling to this truth: *Go back now and Hayley will have a dad for a short time; or stay away, and we could develop a relationship for life.*

I wrote to Sue, explaining what I was trying to do, and she in turn told my family. I wasn't particularly interested in what anyone thought, though. I was dying a slow death, and every attempt I had made to clean up had failed. Opinions meant nothing to me; I needed the right advice and guidance.

Anger

A guy who introduced himself as my counsellor told me that it was going to be a rough road ahead, calling for every ounce of honesty and courage I could muster. He then said the weirdest thing to me: 'And we can have a good look at all that anger' – and with that he walked off. I was speechless. Didn't he realize I had just come from Strangeways Prison? Could he not understand how happy I felt to be out of that hellhole? I thought, 'What is he talking about?'

I was up first the next morning because of the silence. It was deafening. Alex, my cellmate, had snored like a rhino for four months, so now it was so quiet I could not settle. The previous day I had had porridge from hell for breakfast – the stuff to repair shoes with – served by a tattooed bloke from Rochdale. But this morning I was offered a variety of cereal, fresh coffee, fresh orange juice, a mixture of fried goodies and toast, by a lady who seemed to genuinely care. I couldn't handle all the choice and started to feel like I was in the way, so I just scooped a major portion of cornflakes and orange juice and sat down.

My social skills were non-existent. I found that I did not have the inner confidence to ask what I was allowed to have. I felt like I was stealing. It took me something like two weeks before I felt right about helping myself, but I failed to see how significant a role my lack of confidence had played in getting me this far. I had created my own confidence, from a platform of 'If anyone challenges me, I'll fight them.'

The day was built around group and one-to-one counselling sessions, from nine in the morning through to, sometimes, nine at night. Talking about feelings, questioning motives, being forced to look at the effects of one's addiction on family and community members. Every sentence was stripped down and analysed by pretty much everyone. It was in-depth examination of the way we had lived, and motives were tested each day.

I bumped into my counsellor on the stairs and he stopped to greet me and we had a quick chat. As he left he said, 'We will talk about your anger soon.' I was struck dumb again. I looked around to ensure he was talking to me, and then I laughed into empty space. 'That guy is weird!' I thought. 'This is the life of Reilly.'

I was finding the group sessions really deep and heavy. Women were talking about rape and men were talking about raping. People were openly crying with both pain and compassion.

Among all the counselling staff, the Director of Treatment was a limping Irishman named P.J. McCullough, who had survived years of chronic alcoholism. He was a spiritual giant, with a stature one can only attain through suffering of the extreme kind. PJ was gentle yet firm, quiet and wise, and everyone held him in extremely high regard – some to the point of awe.

Whenever he took the group, people were on the edge of their seats, wondering what insights he might have.

At no point, though, did I feel intimidated by this guy. In fact, I often looked at him and inwardly thought to myself, 'I could do what you do.' In the group situation he would read people and anticipate their thought life, and would somehow manage to cut a long story very short. He would go directly to the root of the problem and expose all the reasons and justifications around it, showing everyone how the alcoholism/addiction functioned, and what was required to counter the problem.

I saw that only brutal honesty would do for our brutal problems. A couple of weeks into my treatment, I started to feel very vulnerable. I wrote to Sue about my vulnerability, and asked her to help me by visiting me with Hayley. That was the start of my decline. I was starting to feel vulnerable, and so I turned to someone to fix me.

PJ walked past me in the corridor one day and said, 'Oh, Colin, I keep meaning to talk to you about your anger,' and once again he left me high and dry.

Without him knowing, I swung round and followed him into his office. As he sat down, he saw me and got the fright of his life. I leaned on his desk, looked him in the eye, and through gritted teeth growled, 'Say that once more and I'm going to break your jaw!'

He sat back and simply smiled at me – a lovely warm and friendly smile. He simply said, 'There it is.' I was caught breathless by his loving smile and friendliness in the midst of my attempt to intimidate him.

PJ had gone to work on me as soon as he set eyes on me two weeks before, with a very professional motive of getting me to a place where I would have no defence. He was right; I was the angriest man in that establishment. I had managed, over many years, to develop skills to hide it from everyone, including myself, behind a false confidence and a sense of humour.

I was due back in Crown Court for sentence on 1 August 1992. I was originally scheduled to stay in treatment for fourteen weeks, but the extent of the damage done in the previous twenty-plus years caused my stay to run into seventeen weeks.

Each week the whole house would gather to give someone a 'final peer assessment' before the guy or woman left. Every week was pretty much the same. The graduate had to sit in silence while everyone (twenty or more people) gave feedback to him or her. During our stay, all our ways were examined and tested. It was truthful and direct.

I noticed how everyone seemed to receive the same feedback in one specific area. When the question of what the person should do next was considered, the group feedback was always: 'You really do need to consider going for extended care for a year or so.' The graduates were being told they were not ready to go home yet. I gave that very same feedback week in, week out. This last group session always got very emotional too.

After seventeen weeks of soul-searching and honesty about myself – ten to fourteen hours a day, seven days a week – my final peer assessment group dawned. I went into it feeling reasonably secure. My group work had been impressive; two guys actually commented that when I walked into a session, they reacted like they did when PJ walked in. My one-to-ones with him had also gone very well. I felt one hundred times better than I had done sixteen weeks previously, when those weirdoes met me at the door. I had no inclination towards drugs, and actually felt a sense of compassion towards all those guys in prison who were not getting the opportunity I had been given. I really felt inwardly better about myself and about life ahead.

As we walked into my final group, I noticed a slight difference in format to all the others I had witnessed. It was customary for the counsellor of the graduate to sit next to him or her. As I followed PJ into the big-group room, I saw that another counsellor was right behind me. He just smiled, but in no way reassured me. Something was going on.

The group started as normal. I got excellent feedback from everyone; it could not have been better. Then, when it was PJ's turn, he simply turned to me and said, 'Colin, let's talk about your mum.'

It was like getting slapped in the dark; I had no idea at all it was coming. I seem to remember mumbling something along the lines of, 'If you want to.'

But before I could get my head around it all, he said very forcibly, 'What one word would you want to say to her if she were here right now?'

As he started his attack, as I saw it, I started to rationalize my way out of it in my head, telling myself to humour him. But then I heard another message in my head, simply saying, 'Trust him.' And with that I inwardly relaxed and allowed him in.

In answer to his question, I heard myself saying 'Sorry' – and with it there instantly came an eruption of emotional turmoil bursting up and out of me. I started to weep, and it turned into a sob, and then I sobbed and sobbed, and I then began to kind of howl and wail. Strange noises simply ejaculated out of me. I actually thought to myself at one point, 'Is that me?' My knees came up to my chest and I sat and wept into my lap for about fifteen minutes. It just poured out of me, as years of bottled-up grief found its release. I was aware of repeating the word 'Sorry' to my imaginary mum.

As it started to subside, I became very aware of two things. One was that my jeans were wet through with tears and snot, and the other was that the room was absolutely silent. Eventually, like a tortoise coming out of its shell, I started to straighten up. As I did, I noticed that most of the people were not paying me any attention. They were holding each other and hugging each other.

I then noticed that some of them were crying. As I focused, it dawned on me that almost everyone in the room was crying with me. Not for me, but with me. Certainly all the women were crying, and it looked like some of the men were crying too, and the nursing staff and the counselling staff – everyone was crying! Right at that very moment I received a very deep healing. I was all right – I knew I was all right – and I knew I was loved.

The format of the session then resumed its normal pattern, and these beautiful people began saying good-bye to me. They each then asked me what I was going to do next. In a flash I realized that we were fast heading towards July, and I was up for judgement in August. I knew in my heart that I had changed and that I had received a real healing in my time there. I wanted to go home now and make a new effort at daddying my girl. I looked around that room, and it seemed that each face held hope for me.

When the time came for me to speak, and I was asked, 'What do you think you should do next?', right at the very moment of truth, I replied, 'I think I should go to extended care.' The whole room erupted with applause and people ran to hug me. I got lost in all that emotion for a little while, but within my heart I knew I had just been dishonest. I wanted to go home and truly believed I could make a go of it. I said 'yes' when I meant 'no', in order to please people, and that was the root cause and engine-room of my addictive bondage.

At that point in my treatment I started to relapse, but for twenty minutes or so, I was the man of the moment. Relapse is never an event – it is always the end of a long process, and I went into that process as soon as I started to deny the truth of my heart through fear of rejection. I made contact with Sue again, to let her know how well I was doing. My relapse was in motion now; I started to rebuild bridges back into addiction.

The Cotswolds is undoubtedly one of the most beautiful parts of Europe's countryside. The valleys around Stroud are green and the people are warm and friendly. Early mornings are the most spectacular, as the mist rises up from the valleys and one can see trees sticking out of the top of the mist, and on occasion, a cottage on the other side of the valley might give out a stream of smoke from its chimney-stack. It is absolutely gorgeous.

I travelled from Lancashire to the Cotswolds on the train, deeply disappointed in myself. I wanted to go home, but did not have the gumption to risk saying so in the group situation. I actually went through Stockport on the train, and as I did so I thought of my daughter within a mile of me. Immediately following this line of thought, I was thinking of a heroin supplier who lived between the station and where my daughter was, and that started a craving in me.

The hijacking

I followed through on my promise to go to Nelson House, hoping my heart would get back into recovery mode, but by the time I got to Stroud I knew exactly what I was going to do. I had primed Sue in Stockport; she was ready to have this 'new Colin' back. I got a taxi from the station to Nelson House, and I knocked at the front door. A young guy opened the door, wearing twenty or thirty studs in different parts of his face and sporting a Mohican hairstyle. I can remember thinking from behind a painted smile, 'Wonderful – a zoo!' I was judging people before they had spoken a word to me because of how they looked. It was only a matter of time before I got into a fight.

At night I was lying awake listening to love songs on the radio, and dedicating the really romantic ones to an imaginary lover. I knew all the words of the love songs but had no one to sing them to.

I stayed one week, and totally rejected anything anyone said in the group sessions. People were trying to love me, but I was set on getting them to reject me. I was trapped in the 'Oh, that might be all right for you' syndrome and sitting in arrogant judgement on everyone. I had failed to see that the craving I had stirred up in myself a week earlier was now dominating my attitude towards recovery.[6] I was given good, sound advice and I threw it out without consideration. The impending judgement on 1 August meant nothing to me either by now.

After one week I sabotaged a group session with talk of extreme violence and cruelty. People got up and left. I accused them of rejecting me, grabbed my pre-packed holdall and walked out.

Less then 200 yards from that rehabilitation centre was the entrance to an industrial estate. As I approached this entrance, a truck was slowly exiting. I opened the passenger door and jumped in and said to the very startled driver, 'Drop me off near the motorway, mate!'

He gestured for me to get out of his truck and said, 'I'm not going near the motorway,' slamming on his brakes.

I looked him right in the eyes and growled slowly with tear-filled eyes and clenched teeth, 'Take me to the ******* motorway!'

The guy went white and just said, 'All right, calm down – I can go that way.'

The rest of the journey is a blur to me, but as soon as I got back into Stockport, I just walked back into Sue's life, unpacked my bag, and the next day I went for heroin. I went from Mr Recovery to full-blown addictive attitude in the blink of an eye. Within two days, and with just over a month to go before judgement, I was once again injecting heroin and amphetamines and breaking into houses in broad daylight. Now my thinking was, 'I've just been in one of the best addiction clinics in Europe, and it hasn't worked for me. This time, when I go to prison, my release date will be so far down the line that I won't have to worry about it.'

I somehow made it through the month before court without getting nicked again. On one burglary I found an old man in an unconscious state in his bathroom. He was lying face up, and just by instinct I spun him over onto his belly. He made a very dim groaning noise, so I knew he was alive. I dipped his pockets, believing he would be dead soon anyway and in no need of money, so I took his wallet. I called the police and gave them his details, before spending his money on heroin and using his credit card to get myself some new training shoes for the jail. Once again I made the front page of the *Manchester Evening News*: 'BURGLAR WITH A HEART SAVES MAN'S LIFE'. There was no mention of me robbing him first.

Having been in treatment, I had won back the favour of my dad. However, just before my day at Crown Court, Dad came to visit me, but on his arrival I was in the bathroom at Sue's, injecting sleeping pills following a night on amphetamines. I'd been speeding for three days and needed sleep. I injected seven sleeping pills and then Sue called me to tell me my dad was there. I skipped down the stairs two at a time and into the lounge area, and then just collapsed at his feet. I was rushed to hospital, and once again I woke up in intensive care wired to that very familiar-sounding heart monitor, surrounded by several medics, with a drip in my arm and my hand.

Chapter 5

More Prison

It was 1 August 1992. Judge Bracewell sat in her cloak and wig, glasses perched on the end of her nose. She had good reason to look puzzled. The probation reports on me could not be traced. I spoke up without invitation and said, 'There are no reports, ma'am. I did not report to the Probation Office. I've relapsed. I'm back on drugs.'

'You will go to prison for thirty months.'

I went to the cells at Manchester Crown Court, and it was just like the last six months had been a crazy dream. I lay down on one of the benches, folded my arms over my eyes, crossed my feet, and began once again to think prison. The faces of all the people at the clinic kept me company to begin with, but they soon started haunting me. Now I was back amongst the animals. I smoked a weed that night with a guy who could see the state I was in. The pot did nothing for me. It slowed my mind down, but it could not reach the emotional torment and sense of failure I had within me. In my heart I resolved to end my life at the first available opportunity.

Because the main prison at Strangeways was still being renovated, Manchester prisoners were sent all over the country to serve time. My second night of the thirty months was spent in Nottingham Police Station.

I silently planned my suicide for bedtime that night. A guy doing a lot of laughing on the wing walked past my cell and made a comment about heroin addicts. I had nothing to lose. When the guy went to the loo, I burst in on him and punched him ten or so times as he sat there, stunned. I then returned to my cell and sat there, trembling with fear and rage.

Suicide time

Once the door was locked for the night, none of it would matter. I considered writing notes to my dad and Alan and Linda, but I believed they had no interest in me. I thought of writing a letter to my little Hayley, but could think of nothing of any value to put in it.

I therefore found myself at life's end, totally alone and so convinced that there was no way out, that even the misery felt strangely peaceful. I counted down my 'lasts'. The last cup of tea. The last head count. The last door slamming. The last sliding spy-hole cover. The last bolt.

I tore a strip of sheet off my bedding and sat staring at it for a while. I knew I was going to make front-page news again. I wrapped the sheet tightly around my throat, and got into bed, fully clothed. I started to slowly slip away. I knew I was slipping away. I got to a point where I couldn't hear anything and didn't know if I was breathing or not. In that darkness I could see dots, or tiny bubbles floating around me. It was like looking into a kaleidoscope.

It was then, at that point, that one word went through my mind. It just sort of appeared within my mind's eye. It was as clear as crystal – one word, in bold black capitals: GOD.

A bolt of fear shot through me. I somehow managed to roll off my bed and jump up. I removed that sheet with a deep sense of panic. My thoughts were, 'I cannot face him! I am simply not ready to face God!' All suicidal thoughts were abandoned, and I slipped into an even deeper sense of depression.

My weight dropped to below 55 kilograms (when I normally weigh in at 76). Most people thought that was normal for me because I was always underweight due to the drugs, but this time it was stress and depression. I could not eat properly and my sleep was down to one or two hours a night at best. The next few days were a personal hell, and then another letter came from Sue. I opened it with a sense of dread, knowing I could not pretend any more. I was unable to love without the will to live, and I just wanted to be left alone and forgotten. On opening the letter, I found yet again a new low. She said, 'Colin it is over. I am not going to visit or write. Don't reply.' Her words were in line with my thinking, but it felt like another kick in the soul, and this time I knew I was alone. My appearance said more than I could say, and two guys gave me their Valium that they were getting from the police doctor. Now, for a con to give drugs away is a rarity, but these guys saw my state, and it struck chords of compassion in them.

The next day the guys on the wing started to talk to me about parole. If I could get parole, I would be out in March, they said. These cons really took an interest in my condition. I tried to apologize to the guy I'd attacked in the loo. The guys on the wing did everything they could to help me out of the valley of death I had fallen into. Slowly this parole possibility began to confuse me. I did not want to live, but I did not want to die; I did not want to be in prison, but I did not want to be released. I felt like I was at the very bottom of humanity.

I was moved from Nottingham up to the north-east of England, to a prison called Acklington. I was the only guy in there from Manchester. I hustled for cannabis every night and always managed to get some.

One of the local gangsters challenged me one day about why I was in Acklington, suggesting that I was a child molester or something. Rumours like that have got to be extinguished straight away, or a person could find himself seriously injured. Ten or twelve of the main gangsters would congregate every night in the cell of the one who had challenged me, so when I heard what had been said, I went to the cell. I gently knocked on the door and quickly jumped in and closed the door behind me without locking it. I was face to face with approximately ten pot-smoking gangsters in their own fog-bank of cannabis.

The main guy irritably said, 'What?'

I said to them, 'You lot are in here smoking weed while I'm out there with loads of other guys who have none. I don't get visits, so there's no chance of me getting any weed of my own. I can sell for you and at the same time make a bit for myself.'

There was an uncomfortable silence for a moment or two until one of them chirped up, 'How do we know you are not a child molester? If you've been sent up from Manchester, there must be a reason.'

I was waiting for it and wondering who would say it. I simply said, 'There's only one way you can find out whether or not I'm a nonce. If you want, I'll get my depositions sent in from my solicitor and you can read for yourself about my charges. I don't mind doing that, as long you don't mind getting yours sent in for me to read, because I don't know what you are really in for. Some of you might even be grasses,[7] for all I know.'

I held the main guy's stare for a long moment, smiled and simply shrugged. He started to smile and he said, 'Manc,[8] you've got some front!'

I said, 'It's not front – it's a need for weed!'

I came away from that cell with a pocketful of weed for sale throughout the prison. From that point on I became known as 'the Manc', and the locals (Geordies) were coming to me, in their own jail, for drugs. I was one month into my sentence and I was 10,000 miles away from the clinic and everything those guys had taught me. However, in the quietness of the night I would ponder on every face and every hug and every colourful meal, and I slowly started to sink even deeper into a heavy depression over the loss of the one chance I had been given. I tried working out in the gym and playing soccer, but the sadness within me, together with the heavy sense of failure, was slowly getting all mixed into an absolute dread of the future. The longer this went on, the more drugs I needed. I then started to steal tobacco from the cells of the drug dealers in order to buy my own drugs from the dealers who I had nothing to do with. To be caught robbing another prisoner's cell would mean a severe beating, including broken fingers and knees. To be caught robbing one of the main gangsters' cells would have meant even worse punishment, but my internal turmoil was ever present and needed constant sedation. By mid November I was running riot in my attempts to get drugs.

Two detectives from the Greater Manchester police force came to the prison to interview me regarding unsolved crimes in the Stockport area. This happens to pretty much everyone and includes going through a list of unsolved crimes from police files. If a prisoner confesses to any of them, that crime is removed from the 'unsolved' shelf, thus boosting statistics – but no charges are made. The crime is written off. I was freaked out to be getting a visit until I saw it was the police. These two detectives had travelled almost 300 miles to interview me. I saw an opening and went straight in for the kill. I sat down and said, 'I'm not signing anything, or even going to look at your files. However, if you come back tomorrow with £10 worth of tobacco, I will empty your shelves.' They started getting all moral on me, asking me if I expected them to smuggle contraband into one of Her Majesty's Prisons. I simply said, 'It's up to you,' and walked away. I went straight back to the wing and visited one of the main dealers. He had some amphetamine powder and I bought an eight-ounce deal from him and a two-ounce deal of weed, on the strength of the next day's police visit. I was now in serious debt, and if the police did not turn up I was in trouble with a capital 'T'.

One of the drug dealers I was running for was a little guy who was by no means a gangster. He just happened to be in the position of having a wife who brought him weed every week. I tolerated his bravado to meet my own needs, but I was slowly starting to resent this guy because of the way he spoke to me. The other guys often sat with me and smoked a weed with me, but this little character did actually believe he was better than me. On the day when I bought the amphetamines, in front of twenty or thirty guys he made a comment about me having police visits. I just laughed it off and came back with a sarcastic remark that left people laughing at him. Most of the guys knew me by now and knew I was just an everyday thief. But as the amphetamines took over my mind, I started to imagine what could result from a comment like his, and a dangerous resentment started to stir in me. Somehow, I was going to get back at this plastic gangster.

The police turned up the next day and I sat with them for over an hour. They brought me a file to look at containing details of burglaries committed since my last release from prison, and I started to flick through it. I was astounded at the number of burglaries I recognized, and I went through, ticking those that I knew or even suspected I had done. It worked out that since being released after my third sentence and up to my arrest for this fourth sentence,[9] I had been responsible for somewhere in the region of 400 crimes in the Greater Manchester area! I got more and more emotional as I went through the list.

One of the detectives said, 'We were expecting you to sign some, but not this many. Why?'

I spoke from my heart when I told him, 'So that someone somewhere might get a little peace from the fact that the guy who robbed him or her is now in prison. I just want to say sorry to someone.'

I got my tobacco and cleared my debt with the supplier. But by now I was nurturing a serious resentment towards one man. I was full of bad feelings about myself and my situation, but this guy now started to take centre stage in my mental theatre of revenge.

Solitary confinement

Christmas was coming and I started to want a move closer to Manchester. I asked for a transfer to Risley or Strangeways, but was flatly refused without consideration. As the prison officer laughed at me and threw me out of his office, I knew exactly how I was going to do it. I went to every drug dealer in the prison and asked him for a piece of weed for 'a guy on B Wing' and promised that I would bring the tobacco that evening. I was well trusted by now, so almost everyone who had weed gave it to me.

I went to the plastic gangster last, and actually asked him how much he had. He brought two deals out of his pocket and said, 'This is all I have.' I said I could sell them for him 'right now if you want'. He fell hook, line and sinker; and just to twist the knife a little bit, I really smiled at him and said, 'I really enjoy working for you.' Oh, his ego just exploded in front of me and he promised me a treat when I brought him his tobacco.

It was payday, so I went and bought my own supply of tobacco. It was also laundry day, so the sight of prisoners walking round the prison with a pillowcase stuffed with washing was normal. I had my pillowcase but it was filled with the few pathetic belongings I had. Coming away from the canteen, I had fourteen deals of cannabis, three packets of cigarette papers and two ounces of tobacco in my pocket. I very casually walked across the prison, up to the door of the solitary confinement block, and I booted the door with the sole of my boot.

Within ten seconds two prison officers were at the door expecting some sort of trouble. A governor of some sort was standing in the confinement block and I spoke over the officers' shoulders so that he could hear me and I said, 'My life is in danger and I need protection!' They had no choice but to respond, and I was ushered in and put into a solitary confinement cell and the door was slammed behind me.

I erupted with laughter, punching the air and whooping with a twisted form of delight. I bounced up and down on my bed like a six-year-old. I had a pocket full of drugs – enough to last me a week at least. I would now be shipped out and back to Manchester by Christmas, and I had looked the plastic gangster in the eye and ripped him off. Ripping him off was secondary to the pleasure I got from knowing that he would think of me in the quiet of the night, insulting him with a smile. I raised my middle finger in the direction of the main prison from that solitary confinement cell, and started to fantasize about how good life was going to become.

The next day was Friday, so I knew not to expect a ship-out before the weekend, as they only happened on Tuesdays. But my sights were set on being among familiar fools within a week, with glory stories of ripping off the Geordies.

By 2 a.m. I had smoked all the drugs I had come in with. I knew I was smoking a decent standard of weed, but it was not actually having any effect on me. My internal frustrations, failures and fears were impossible to quell. I had a deep and painful remorse continually stirring in me regarding my past. I hated being where I was, and the future was non-existent. And then all of a sudden, I was out of drugs.

I slept a little that first night of solitary. The next morning, when my cell opened, I was absolutely stunned to see a Roman Catholic priest standing in my doorway with a prison officer. I immediately said, 'What do you want?' He began to explain his role in my life as a prisoner in solitary confinement. He got as far as telling me that God loved me, and if ever I needed to talk to him (the priest), all I had to do was say so, because he would be the first face I saw every morning. I cut him off at that point by pushing my door closed and telling him: 'Go and play with yourself, mister – you'll be the last person I talk to!' The door was quickly slammed from the outside and I was suddenly standing with my back to it, finding myself inexplicably wanting to cry. I had resolved in my heart not to talk to 'these clowns', or the other prisoners in solitary confinement, because they were child molesters and rapists, and this aggressive isolation would also speed up the ship-out.

I had a little radio for in-house entertainment with a new battery that would last me until I got out of that hellhole, and there were several books in the cell for me to read. I would not use the daily one-hour exercise time, because that meant interaction with the perverts. I tried to make the battery last so that I could have the late-night love-song station on the radio to torment myself by reminding myself that I had no one to dedicate any of the songs to.

It was in those times that I started to feel something very heavy bearing down on me. It was like a very long, wet, heavy trenchcoat was being placed on me, but always getting heavier and heavier. I would walk up and down my cell and get a crushing sensation all around me. I had no drugs to sedate me, and no one to talk to. And then the penny dropped – it was the silence and the loneliness that was crushing me. My past was continuously attacking me with both good and bad memories. I had the faces of my circle of friends from the clinic flashing through my mind, quickly followed by the names and faces of guys I had bonded with who were all now dead from drugs. I started making a list one day of the names of the people I had known who were now dead from addiction. I abandoned it after thirty minutes or so because I was afraid of forgetting someone. It haunted me to know that this was where I was heading. It was the thought of no one turning up for my funeral that ate away at me the most. Painful thoughts about my mum resurfaced and twisted in my heart like a knife. And I had not yet spent even one weekend in solitary.

Tuesday came and went and there was not even the mention of me being shipped out. By Thursday I was longing for someone to talk to. I was bursting with nervous energy and started to run up and down my cell, on the bed, off the bed, kicking the door and yelling all kinds of obscenities at the world. Whenever a screw came to the door I would be stood against the door, panting and sweating and totally enjoying his interaction with me. I would get called all kinds of names by the screws, but I just laughed them off with enjoyment at being recognized as existing. I would then swing from this crazy euphoric high to sitting on my bed with a pillow pressed up against my face in an effort to keep the sobbing noises down to a minimum.

After one week of what felt like total solitude, I took up the offer of going out into the eighteen-feet-square exercise yard with the two other prisoners. One of them was obviously missing a slate or two and unable to hold a two-way conversation. The other was a bald-headed guy who looked quite normal to my company-starved eyes, and I got alongside him. We walked in this stupid circle for a full hour and both of us talked the whole time. We spoke over each other. He was having one conversation about his life and I was having another about mine. Loneliness does the strangest things to a man's mind. Towards the end of my self-centred hour, I managed to get a response from him when I asked how long he had been in solitary. He looked at me through unnaturally grey eyes, the same colour as his skin, and said, 'Fourteen years on and off.' I was dumbstruck. One week had nearly crushed me, and this guy had made a life out of it. It turned out he could never settle in mainstream prison because he was a baby killer.

That night I sat staring at the wall for hours and I had to concede that this guy had, from time to time, seemed very normal to me. I actually thought to myself that there was very little difference between him and me, and I began to see that this individual's circumstances had twisted and crushed and moulded him into what he had become, and it was only a matter of pot luck that it was him and not me. And that being the case, what on earth was I becoming? I was bad enough when I came to prison; where the hell was I going next – especially having now sunk to my current depth of self-hatred?

The future went from black to blacker still. My parole date was three months away, and my full-term release date was fifteen months away. The thought of release scared me, but it was from the possibility of parole that I got my only sense of hope. Christmas seemed to gallop towards me, and I asked if I could have a phone call on the grounds of not having had a visit. I had started to accumulate phone cards from my first week in solitary with a view to buying weed with them as soon as I joined mainstream jail again, and offered to surrender them for a chat to my daughter on Christmas Day. I was given the phone call and allowed to keep my cards.

Hayley and I simply said we loved each other over and over again, and that night I slept very soundly. I had no promises to make to her, because I really did not know if I was going to live through this sentence. The New Year crept in very quietly for me, although I was lying awake listening to the main prison erupting in whistles and howls as the midnight minutes passed. It was now 1993 – would I see it through?

Shortly into the New Year, my cell door opened and one of the staff looked in and said, 'Sorry, son – your parole application has been turned down,' and he closed the door very quietly. I fell onto my bed and released a huge sigh of relief. I felt a huge burden lift from me, and I relaxed for the first time in months. I could actually see the insanity of my wanting to stay in prison, but that was just the way it was for me. My past was too painful to look at. My present was a constant struggle for survival. My future was non-existent. I did not want to live. I did not want to die. I hated prison. I feared release. You work it out!

Mainstream prison

My transfer came not long after my parole refusal and I was slipped back into the mainstream prison population. I wanted to talk to everyone I met. My phone cards lasted me two days. I used one to call Hayley and the other six went on weed. Before I left solitary I signed the wall. It's a prison thing. I wrote my name, where I was from, what I was in for and the jails I had been in. I then noticed that I had been in eleven different prisons in my relatively short prison career. I felt a deep sense of sadness about my miserable journey so far, not knowing that it was about to get much worse. I had had a lot of thinking time in solitary and could see quite clearly that I had to change my circle of friends, because every one of my current friends was drug-involved. I felt inwardly sure that if I could just get a new start somewhere 'away from the madding crowd', I could make a go of it in life drug-free.

But whilst I was having these thoughts, I was saving phone cards to buy some weed as soon as I got back into mainstream prison! I was suffering from a very selective amnesia that I regularly used. I not only made the right noises to impress other people, but I also made them to impress myself. I actually believed that my intentions would dictate my behaviour. I knew there was a prison right on the south coast of England, and I fantasized that there no one would know me and I could escape from the trap of reputation and the pull towards the drug culture, from which I was an outcast.

I started heading back towards the north-west England prisons, stopping off at several places like HMP Armley in Leeds and Walton in Liverpool, and finally ending up in Wymott near Preston. Arriving at Wymott created a new pit in my emotional and spiritual valley. I went to a new low at this point. My dad visited me and asked me to release my part of the ownership of the house that we jointly owned to my step-mother. Dad and I had purchased the house whilst I was still in the Army, for my future. When Dad and Maureen had announced that they were going to get married several years earlier, I had said to Alan, 'She will get the house from me.' My robbing them gave her all the ammunition she needed, and now they wanted to sell and move to Portland in Dorset.

I felt an immense sense of guilt and loneliness about them selling that house. I knew that I had spoiled it for them as a home by robbing them. As I signed the deed over to them, I tried to catch my dad's eye to maybe offer some sort of apology, but he avoided me. I just scribbled on the forms. It meant nothing to me anyway; I just hated the fact that it was her influence behind it all. I was extremely resentful towards Maureen and made no secret of it to the rest of my family. But then I realized that I could capitalize on my dad living in Dorset, if I played my cards right. If I kept writing to him at his Portland address, as if everything was sweet between us, I could apply for a transfer to that area of the country on the grounds of place of residency on release.

'WYMOTT' stands for 'Where You Must Obey The Tannoy'. There is a marked absence of prison staff in Wymott because prisoners cannot escape the Tannoy system and are called for if and when needed. This pretty much meant that the prisoners ran the prison as they wanted. I witnessed several vicious beatings in the internal drug wars of Wymott. One could visit a guy in his cell before supper and all would be well. On return after supper, he would be lying there unable to move because rival gang members getting revenge for some drug-related or woman-related issue had smashed his knees and ankles. There was no telling who would be next.

I was very nervous in Wymott because I had been in solitary, and many prisoners often put two and two together and come up with three. If these characters found out that I'd been down the block, someone would conclude that I was either a nonce or a police informer, and I could be next. Wymott was a mix of mainly Manchester and Liverpool prisoners, and there has always been a vicious competitiveness between these two cultures. I suppose it is because of the two cities holding four of the main soccer clubs in the English Premier League, but it also spreads into prison politics.

I was in with eight or nine guys from my area of Stockport, and we were pretty much left alone and respected. Chris Little was among our number and he was one of the most feared bullies ever to come out of Stockport. Chris just fell short of a professional boxing career because he failed to cope with guys actually hitting him back, and so he transferred his 'skill' onto the streets, where most of us were smaller than him. Chris became known for his jaw-breaking punch and was quoted as saying, 'I am going to knock everyone with a reputation clean out.'

He was training in his garden one afternoon, and I was holding the medicine ball for him to work out on. He was big, strong and fast. Following one of his training sessions one day, he flexed himself in front of me and then said exactly what was in my mind: 'All it will take is some dirty little junkie to put a gun to my head and go "Bang!"', and he faked being shot. Chris is now buried in Stockport cemetery with the epitaph 'At Peace in God's Kingdom' on his headstone, because some young guy apparently drew up alongside him at some traffic-lights one day in Stockport and blew the side of his head off with both barrels.

A similar sort of character came onto the scene from among the Liverpool contingent in Wymott shortly after Chris Little got out. This guy was 19 or 20 years old, was 6 feet 2 inches tall, and had the body of a world-class athlete and the speed of a professional fighter. He was frightening even to look at, and he was on a rampage, taking drugs off people by force. No one could stop him. I had been at Wymott about three weeks, and one night I went to the cell where our little gang would meet and smoke together. As I walked in, someone said to me, 'Colin, you could take this guy out if you put your mind to it.' I knew whom they were talking about, and I also agreed with them, but my confidence was shot to pieces. I was 15 kilos underweight and the thought of this guy had kept me awake more than once. What came out of my mouth was the exact opposite of the truth. I simply said, 'I'm going to.' In a split second of hot air, I had committed myself to a mission impossible from which these guys would not let me back down. I went back to my cell that night and wondered what the hell I had said.

The next day I knew exactly what I was going to do. I was doing a welding course at Wymott and saw this guy most mornings. I went out of my way to give him a jail style of respect on my way to work that day, and he, obviously desperate for friends, returned my greeting with an equal amount of this prison counterfeit admiration. Straight away I knew I had him, and I put my plan into motion.

I told no one what I was doing, but he became an obsession for me. I took a piece of metal from one side of the welding shop, another piece from another, and welded them together in my secluded welding booth. I then sharpened one end until it was extremely sharp. I hid the six-inch blade in another guy's cell without him even knowing, and went about my day like everything was normal. Only now I was openly greeting this guy and even approached him for weed on one occasion.

After a week or so, I knew I had him. I got the blade to my cell, and took it to work with me the next day. My plan was to get up alongside the guy that evening when work finished and everyone was out and about, and get him comfortable with me. I was going to ram it in behind his knee and yank it up to the buttock, making sure he would not be able to chase me, whilst simultaneously ensuring that if he died it would not be murder because of the place of entry, and ensuring he would never return onto mainstream Wymott. Only I knew. I had the blade up my sleeve, knowing that I had him the next time I saw him. I felt very calm; similar to the way I had felt about my suicide before God interrupted.

As I was looking for him, there was a skirmish on one of the wings and bells started to ring. We were all returned to cells. When the storm passed there was a buzz all over the prison. Two guys from Wales had jumped my target and almost put him on a life-support machine in the prison hospital.

I found it difficult to walk back to my cell because of my trembling. I felt physically sick with the release of tension. I sat in my cell, and I was cold with anger at myself. I was going to stab this guy, 'for them'. I was going to end up with a possible fifteen-year sentence, 'for them'. It was all 'for them', for the approval of the crowd.

The next day I went into the wing office and I asked for a transfer. I had to get away from this hellhole.

The screw said, 'Transfer to where?'

I said, 'The Verne.' This was the jail on the south coast of England.

The screw actually laughed at me. He said, 'Son, we would all like to go to The Verne, but the Dorset prison service and the county council won't take a heroin addict from Manchester, to be released into their community, especially two days before Christmas!'

Everything he said made sense, but as he finished talking I said, 'Am I allowed to apply?'

He said, 'Oh, you can apply.'

I said, 'I want to apply.'

I made the application and stayed off work that day to have the second interview with the governor about the request. I was called into the governor's office and asked to make my case known. I was asked why I wanted to go to The Verne.

I looked straight at the governor and said to him, 'Sir, your prison is full of heroin. I am a heroin addict and I am not changing. I have to get as far away from this part of the country as I possibly can, and I am trying to build a new relationship with my dad. I have only just starting writing to him again in recent weeks. I write to him regularly now and would like to go and live with him when I get out. I am doing everything in here that I have been doing outside for the past seventeen years, and it is killing me from the inside. Sir, when this prison goes up in flames, I want nothing to do with it or the people involved.'

I welled up with tears at this point because of the truth within my fabrication. The room went very quiet. I said, 'I know in my heart, Sir, that if you could see the turmoil going on in me, you would take officialdom off and the gentleman in you would say "Go."'

He sat quietly for the best part of a minute. I simply walked out before he responded. I could not quite fathom why I had mentioned the prison going up in flames, but giving it some after-thought, it could not be ruled out. Wymott was a pressure cooker always on the boil.

I knew from experience that a prison transfer request takes between eight and twelve weeks in many cases. The application is studied and considered by the sending prison, including checking where my letters have been addressed, and then considered by the requested prison; then the forms are sent to the Home Office in London where they join a pile waiting to be considered and then stamped 'yes' or 'no', before returning to the sending prison.

I came out of the governor's office that day, with all my ducks in a row, and I just knew in my heart that I was going to The Verne. As I returned to the wing, the laughing screw was stood in his office doorway, but now it was me doing the laughing. I said, 'Ask me who is going to The Verne.' He would not ask. I did wonder what was going through my dad's mind as he received all my letters of reconciliation, but knowing him, I guessed he would know that I was up to something.

I went into work for the remainder of the morning; I was also on afternoon education classes at this time, in which I took an English exam for fun. I really enjoyed using my brain and I actually got a distinction for my exam.

As I returned to the wing that same day for lunch, two hours after my meeting with the governor, he called me into his office. He sat me down and simply said, 'Your name is on the list for transfer to The Verne next Thursday. Do not ask me how or why, but your name is on this list for the bus to Reading en route to HMP The Verne' – and he gestured me out of his office. I went back to my cell that day very slowly. I spoke to no one. As I was sitting on my bed that day, I knew, with a deep and really weird assurance, that a miracle had occurred in my life. My mind very nearly drifted towards God again, but that was ridiculous, and I snapped myself out of it, but not before thinking that I would have actually got the transfer, even without the manipulative mail games.

It was May 1993; summer was just around the corner, and one week later I would be climbing onto a nice clean southbound mini-bus. I had a whole new feeling taking over me from that point: hope. Something either unnatural or supernatural had happened for me the day I cried out over my hopeless condition and desire to change in the governor's office. Although I had no clue what was going to happen next, I knew one thing – life was drifting from black to grey. It was almost starting to look better.

The journey to Dorset was a long one and we stopped off at five or six other prisons before we got to Winchester for a final stop before The Verne. I had smoked a weed on the way down with some guys, but felt a sense of shame about it. My heart's cry had been 'I am not changing', and here I was, being given a chance, and I still wasn't changing. I had a single cell for my brief stop at Winchester, and all through that night I was preparing myself for my arrival at The Verne. I told myself, 'I must avoid the drug culture, maybe get involved in church and the gym, do education classes, either find clean friends or have no friends.' I was deeply excited because I felt inwardly different this time. I knew I could do this. I'd been in good rehabs and Europe's finest clinics; now it was up to me. I had seven months left to serve, and with this final glimpse of hope, I felt that all might not be lost.

On the bus to The Verne the next day, I was handcuffed to a guy who was returning there. He was a lifer and had been to London on accumulated visits.

As we got going, for some weird reason I asked him, 'What is the Christian fellowship like at The Verne?'

He smiled and said, 'On fire.'

I started to relax.

Fear of release

Travelling to Portland, the peninsula sticking out from Weymouth in Dorset, upon which The Verne is located, I was feeling inwardly sad because of my memories. As a family, before all the madness started, we used to come to Weymouth for our annual holiday. Mum, Dad, Alan, Linda and myself; and now here I was cuffed to a lifer, heading for my twenty-sixth prison, seventeen years into an unstoppable intravenous heroin and amphetamine addiction.

Reception at The Verne held one officer and three prisoners who did all the booking in and kit-issue. The prison officer spoke with a lovely soft Dorset accent, and his attitude was much softer than the northern screws. He spoke to me and offered suggestions, whereas the northerners spoke at me and barked orders. One of the cons asked me where I had come from and when I told him Wymott, he asked if I was one of the rioters. I asked him what he meant and he explained that Wymott had been burning for the last three days. I was very close to saying 'Thank God', but that was ridiculous.

When the prison officer had finished all the in-house rules, he asked me, 'Do you prefer a single cell?' I was mind-blown, but the best was yet to come. I asked for a single cell and was given the wing and cell number written on a piece of paper, and a key! I thought I was on candid camera. We had our own keys! The door into the main prison was then opened and the officer said, 'Go and find your cell, get unpacked and settled in, then tomorrow go and find yourself a job or a training course.'

The Verne is a training prison and offers training in different areas and skills. I walked around the jail, unchallenged, until I found my cell. The windows did not have bars; guys had curtains up and plants in their cells; and not only was the place clean, but one could see the sea from the wing. I found my cell and started to move in. The rest of the wing was at work, so I started cleaning out the cell from the last guy.

As I emptied the drawers, I found a cannabis pipe. Without thinking, I looked through the barrel of the pipe and found it was thick with oil. Within minutes I had snapped a length of thread from my bed-cover, tied three cigarette papers to one end, passed the other end through the pipe, warmed the barrel of the pipe for a few seconds and then pulled the papers through. What came out were three cannabis-oil-saturated cigarette papers, and I proceeded to roll a joint. Within five minutes of being in my new cell, with my new plan of avoiding the drug culture because it kept leading me astray, I was smoking a joint strong enough to knock a donkey over! When the rest of the guys came back to the wing for their lunch, they were met by a fog-bank of cannabis coming out off my cell, and the drug culture gravitated towards me.

The insights and information about addiction during my time at the clinic started to resurface in me at this point, and although I had failed to stay clean, I started to use clinic terminology among the guys who were coming to my cell to either sell or find weed. I started to talk about 'dealing with the feelings', 'considering the consequences of drugs' and 'taking responsibility for past actions and reactions'. But all the time, I was ensuring that I had a little sorter for bedtime. I got myself onto a painting and decorating course and tried to occupy my mind in that way, but each day I would have to walk past the main gate just as that day's discharges were leaving the prison, and the fear of release started to stir within me.

I had gravitated towards a certain table in the dining-room where a guy from Scotland used to sit on his own. It turned out that this guy, Steve, from Motherwell, was a regular churchgoer in the jail. Steve liked a weed and from time to time I would go to his cell and have a smoke with him. Invariably the conversation would drift towards the Bible and I would question him from behind a fog-bank of weed, and analyse the answers with arrogance and cynicism.

Haunted by the Holy Ghost

On 17 June 1993, however, I woke up at the normal time of 7:30 a.m., but something was different. I could not pin down what it was, but something was different. I was trying to get up and get dressed, but my mind was continuously attracted to the name of Jesus. I could not think of anything else other than the name of Jesus. I did get up and get dressed, I shaved and cleaned my teeth, but all the time I had the name of Jesus going through my mind. I went down for breakfast and held conversations with people but all the time, going on in my background, I could hear the name of Jesus in a very quiet but never-drowned-out whisper – *Jesus Jesus Jesus Jesus* – on and on, over and over.

I went to my painting and decorating with it – *Jesus Jesus Jesus Jesus*. The Golden Hour was on Radio 1 for all of us to listen to as we decorated our allocated rooms, and the daily norm was for us to sing along and guess what the year was. Most of us identified tunes by means of what jail we were in when it was out, but this day, for me, was different. *Jesus Jesus Jesus Jesus*. By lunchtime I was almost used to it and was quietly enjoying something no one else had experienced. It was weird to my mind, but kind of soothing to my soul.

I took my lunch to my cell, and after eating it I went for a walk to Steve's cell. I was in no way expecting him to give me an answer, because it did not take a genius to work out that this was something beyond standard man's understanding. However, I approached Steve with it. I explained everything to him from the moment I had woken knowing something to be different. Steve had a beautiful glow about him as he looked at me that day, and as he did so, he seemed to speak right into the very soul of me when he said, 'Colin, Jesus is calling you.'

Steve's answer cut right through me and from somewhere within my empty existence, I just knew he was right. Just like I had known that a miracle had taken place, and just like I had known that I was going to the Verne, and just like I had known Wymott was going to go up in smoke. Beyond my human mind, I knew Jesus was calling me.

I had grown up with a dad who ruled by the tone of his voice, and I had felt his wrath many times. I had been up before a couple of Military Courts Martial, in front of the most frightening of disciplinarians, and I had felt their wrath. I'd been bullied by the toughest military gym instructors that the British Army had to offer, and very nearly been broken within their torture. I'd seen the whites of the eyes of IRA terrorists in Belfast, and virtually smelled the stale ale on their breath as they smiled at the idea of my murder. I'd broken into gangsters' houses, even stood at the side of their beds whilst they slept, and then walked away with their gold. I'd robbed a police station whilst the police were attending a traffic accident outside their station. I'd gone on one-man missions in jail that no one in their right mind would even consider. I'd been shot at, shouted at, and pushed around by the best in the business. Fear actually energized me, but nothing struck fear into my soul like the idea of Jesus Christ inclining his attentions in my direction and actually 'calling me'.

This brought home to me the fact that simply by virtue of my attitude and life-style, I was his enemy. I agreed with everything I had heard about him and the things he had said in the Bible, and I sympathized with how he was crucified and all that stuff, but I had absolutely no desire at all in me to get personal with him. I was comfy with him at arm's length, or in the manger at Christmas, but no more. Steve said to me, 'There is a baptism in the chapel tonight. Are you coming?' I walked off shaking my head, actually having to hold the wall in order to walk in a straight line. I was steadfast in how I was definitely not going to the chapel that night. In fact, it was Thursday and I was the organizer of the Narcotics Anonymous group, so the chapel was a no-no!

The rest of that afternoon is a blank to me. I cannot recall whether or not the *Jesus Jesus Jesus* thing went on into the afternoon. However, what did happen that evening will never leave me. I left my cell with a box of literature for the NA Group, with a view to setting up for the meeting. Now what happened to that box is a mystery to me. I can only imagine that I gave it to someone to stand in for me, but I do not remember. As clear as crystal, though, I do remember walking towards the chapel that night, and seeing Christian prisoners from each corner of the jail walking to that house of God in twos and threes. It was one of the most beautiful sights I had ever seen. It was so peaceful. I had actually reached a point of my life where I cared very little what was about to happen, because the glimmer of hope of which I had caught a glimpse in recent months was slowly fading with every joint I smoked. I walked into that chapel that night, a desperate soul in need.

Chapter 6

Conversion to Christ

As I entered the chapel, I was shocked to see a bright blue industrial rubbish bin sitting in the corner of the room. It was in the wrong place. It was usually reserved for the backs of factories or shops, and wheeled out on refuse collection day. It dominated my view as I walked into that chapel, and I went and sat next to it out of curiosity. It was full of water, though I had no idea why. I sat down and just tried to blend in. Steve was in there with a big daft smile on his beautifully glowing face and I purposely avoided his gaze. Off to my right, there were between twelve and fourteen prisoners, including the lifer I had been cuffed to on the way in.

It turned out that we were waiting for the Prison Christian Fellowship to arrive with guitars and tambourines, and hopefully some biscuits. There was an uncertain silence in the place until a huge black guy stood and started to talk. I made an instant judgement on this guy as being 'ugly'. He had nothing going for him, in my eyes – he was black and he was ugly. However, when he started to speak, I had to check it was his voice. His voice sounded really comforting, almost silky. I was astounded. He said, 'We are waiting for the Christians to arrive, and Jesus himself is here.' He then started to sing the most wonderful song. It went from wonderful to heavenly when the rest of the guys stood up with him and joined in with perfect harmony. They were singing 'Majesty'. It seemed to fill the whole room and was quite tear-provoking.

The PCF arrived in the midst of the singing and initially crept in to listen to the guys singing, but soon got caught up in it themselves. I suddenly became an observer. Steve was as caught up in this rapturous worship as everyone else, but I stood watching, feeling left out and left behind. As the worship grew in volume and adoration, I grew more and more distant from the whole evening.

Twenty minutes or so into the evening a guy, who turned out to be the preacher, stood up and went to the front to deliver a message. He started to talk and read from the Bible, and what he said gave me reason to think that Steve had spoken to him about me, because everything he said pointed to me. I sat there feeling like everyone knew he was talking about me, and I tried to catch Steve's eye, because I wanted to tell him he was out of order talking to these people behind my back. Steve knew all about my failed attempts at cleaning up and what I called 'the clinic failure', and it was more than obvious that the whole night was pointing at me.

The preacher read from Romans 7:15: 'I do not understand what I do. For what I want to do I do not do, but what I hate I do.' Straight away I thought, 'Oh, very funny!' and I tried to catch Steve's eye. It went on: 'I know that nothing good lives in me, that is, in my sinful nature. For I have the desire to do what is good, but I cannot carry it out' (v. 18).A lot of it went over my head, but a lot of it hit me in the very depth of me. And then when he said: 'Who can set me free from this body of death?', he was speaking the language of my heart, and it slowly started to dawn on me that this was some guy in the Bible, with the exact same problems as me. I was stunned by the truth, and the truth seemed to ask me, 'Colin, who is going to rescue you from your body of death?'

From a room in the corner of the chapel, a guy from Jamaica was brought out with a bathrobe on and he was walked towards me. As he got closer, several Christians got up and followed him over to my corner. They were all smiling and hugging this guy, and he then removed the bathrobe. He was wearing a T-shirt and shorts, and he climbed into the bin right next to me and knelt down. Christians crowded into the corner, around the bin and myself, and they started to pray for him.

After a short time, the preacher guy said to everyone in the room, 'Our brother Earl has lived a life displeasing to both God and man. But tonight Earl is openly turning his back on his former lifestyle and turning to God for forgiveness, in Jesus' name.' He then focused on Earl and asked him these three questions out loud:

'Do you believe in your heart that Jesus Christ is the Son of God, that he was crucified for your sin, died and was buried, and after three days was raised from the dead?'

Earl openly confessed this to be his belief.

In my heart I said to myself, 'I've always believed that.'

'Do you confess yourself sinful before God and man, and turn to him with your life and with your soul for forgiveness, confessing Jesus is Lord?'

Earl openly asked God for forgiveness and openly confessed, 'Jesus is Lord.'

I had no doubt about my sinfulness, and from deep within I was crying, 'Jesus is Lord!'

'Do you open your heart now, Earl, and receive Jesus to be your personal Lord and Saviour?'

Earl openly invited Jesus into his heart and life as his own personal Lord and Saviour.

I knew I had never made a personal invitation or commitment to Jesus as the Christ of my life. In fact, my last genuine interaction with God was back on the school stairs, when I aggressively threw the God of my so-called religion into the bin.

Earl was baptized in the name of the Father, and of the Son, and of the Holy Ghost, and he was dunked into the water. The singing erupted once again and people were crying with Earl. I was in a stunned silence. The Christians started to disperse back to their seats, and the preacher went back to his Bible. He threw a gauntlet down to me when he asked, 'Is there anyone else here tonight who feels the need to receive Jesus into their life as personal Lord and Saviour?'

The question had not completely left the minister's lips, and I was standing up and taking my jeans off. I heard myself saying, 'I do! That's exactly how I feel!'

The whole congregation turned to look at me and as they all looked at me, I felt an inner urge to turn it all into a joke and to sit back down. But the truth was, I could no longer live my life under the influence of what other people thought of me. I looked at them, and in a moment's clarity of heart, I knew that I could not allow these guys to define me any longer.

I said, 'I need to know this Jesus for myself.'

My jeans went one way, my shirt went another, and I climbed into this trash can of water and tearfully fell to my knees. I suddenly found myself up to my armpits in water. I thought to myself, 'If this does not work now, I am dead.' However, I then conceded within my heart, 'Actually, I'm already dead.'

Within minutes I was openly confessing my belief that Jesus is the Son of God and that he died on the cross for me and that God raised him from the dead. I was openly confessing myself sinful before God and man, and openly turning to God with grief in my heart over my sin. I turned to him for forgiveness and readily confessed my desire for Jesus to be my Lord. I openly invited Jesus into my heart as my personal Lord and Saviour.

I was then immersed into the waters of baptism.

In the waters, I put my life at the feet of God. To summarize, I said to God in my heart: 'Lord, there is nothing in me of any value. I come before you tonight not knowing who I am. I need you to tell me who I am, and I need release from this inner drive towards destruction. If you are willing, and you make me clean, Lord Jesus, I will serve you with everything that I am for as long as you want me to live, and I do not care what that might mean. If you release me, I am yours lock, stock, and barrel. Lord, in truth, you should actually turn your back on me now; I have no argument. But before you do, I want you to know this: I am truly, deeply sorry for the way I have lived my life.'

Jesus met this junkie exactly where I had left him – in the trash can.

As I came up out of the water, it was as if a heavy, wet trench-coat was removed in that instant. I knew, deep within me, that I had just been saved.

A free man

I was a free man. My addiction ended right at that moment. It was removed. I simply knew it was over. I knew in a second that I had been changed from within, and I knew without counsel that I would never have to take drugs again. I looked towards a guy standing nearby and I expected him to say, 'I saw that!' – such was my feeling of release. I knew that I had been born again, with a rebirth taking place in my heart, in the very soul of me, and that I had literally been transferred from darkness to light.

Christians wanting to pray for me surrounded me, and to begin with it was quite nice, but I must say that my only desire was to be alone with the Lord. A little old lady with eyes alight for God took me by the hand that night and whispered in my ear, 'Barnabas.' Mrs Irene Long from Weymouth Baptist Church made a special point of bringing me worship tapes and giving me my first Bible, and she was the source of wonderful blessings as I started my walk as a new man, in a personal relationship with God.

I somehow removed myself from the chapel that night and made my way back to my cell. I noticed that the light was still on in the education block and the NA group was still running. I went in just as it was ending and made my first confession of Jesus. I apologized to the group for not fulfilling my duty, and then explained that I had just given my heart to Jesus, and would be serving him from here on in. The guys seemed very pleased for me, but I instantly picked up on how the Name of Jesus actually disturbed them.

I went to my cell in a bit of a hurry, because I had a job to do. As I left the chapel, I simply knew what I had to do. My cell wall was heavily stained with worldly pictures of women and I had to remove them and get my heart right with God. I suddenly felt embarrassed about the pictures on my wall. I did not look at any of them when I entered my cell. I kept my eyes lowered, and systematically removed each picture, praying over each one as I did so. Oh boy, had I changed! I asked the Lord to forgive me and to touch the girls in the pictures, that they too would come to repent and be saved. My whole vocabulary had undergone a radical transformation, and my mind was in a process of renewal. My innermost desires had changed and I felt a deep and wonderful sense of peace within the very core of me. It was like a raging storm had been replaced by a clear and still pond.

I sat on my bed that night and simply sat with the Lord. I just sat in the silence, knowing that I was in the presence of the Lord Jesus Christ himself, and that he had been awakened in my storm and had commanded the waters to 'be still'. I suddenly saw how he had even arranged that I lose my share of the house, in order to secure the move to Dorset, in order to get me into a trash can. Losing ownership of that house was for me one of the final straws that broke the camel's back. As long as I had any ownership of that property, I had some measure of control over my life and over other people's lives. It all had to be removed, in order to get me to my knees.

I was free. Jesus had set me free. It was true. That night I got into my bed at about 9:45 p.m., and I prayed for ten or fifteen minutes, and then I went out like a light and slept right through the night to 7:15 a.m. I woke up and lay very still. I wondered if 'it' had vanished in my sleep, but was immediately aware of a wonderful bright new day and a song of joy in my heart. The sky looked different now, because I knew the Architect; the scream of the seagulls sounded totally different now that I knew their Designer. It was so fulfilling to wake up free.

I then realized that I had slept for a full night without interruption. I could not remember ever sleeping right through like that, not even as a child; but now I was free. As I washed, I noticed my eyes had changed. I stood staring at myself in the mirror. My eyes had changed in some way; they were different, and there was a very warm smile within them. I bent to wash and I kept popping back up to check my eyes out because they had changed. My entire thought life, as I prepared to go into my decorating course, revolved around Jesus Christ. He had actually thought about me, and knowing me, he had saved me! I was saved and in Christ. I was born again by the Spirit of Christ. His life in me was now giving me newness of life, and it was a life that no one could take away.

I felt different, but I did not feel like a different person. I felt like I had become the person God had intended me to be, and suddenly I felt a wonderful peace about myself. I was still Colin Garnett, but now I was the true Colin Garnett, born of the Spirit of God. It went on all morning and it was absolutely wonderful.

Halfway through my first new day, I prayed this prayer: 'Lord, should you desire to remove your Spirit from me later today, I would not concern myself about it. I have met you, I know you are alive, and I know you have paid the punishment for the salvation of my soul in the eternal scheme of things.' That night I was still free.

The name of Jesus

On the Sunday afternoon, as most of the prison slept, I crept into the television room and turned the TV on and turned the sound down. I was answering an inner compulsion to see the name of Jesus on the television screen. I knew *Songs of Praise* was on, and I knew they gave subtitles to all their songs. His name caused me to well up with an immense joy. Just the sight of his name on the screen caused me to want to cry. The sight of the singing Christians caused me to want to run around the room and punch the air as if I had scored the winning goal in a cup final. I sat there with a celebration beyond description taking place in my heart. I sat panting and breathless, from simply seeing the name of my Saviour Jesus on the telly, and my new family celebrating him. I belonged, and I knew deep within my heart that I truly belonged, at last.

Guys would see me in the TV room and come in to see what was on. When they realized what I was doing, they would simply stare at me, and then walk out. Some guys went away and came back with one or two others to see this guy from the drug scene with tear-filled eyes, staring at a silent picture of a church. I wanted to try and explain about the power and grace of Jesus to save sinners, but did not have the vocabulary to do so. Collectively they started to mock me. But as individuals, 95 per cent of them came to my cell to see what had happened to me.

All I could tell them at that point was: 'Jesus has set me free.' I could not back my statement up with anything more theological than that. I simply said what I knew: 'Jesus the Son of God tracked me down to my state of nothingness, in a trash can, and liberated me from my body of death, even whilst I was still sinning!'

The academics tried to explain it; the cynics tried to trash it; the philosophers patronized me; and the Muslims simply watched. The prison staff said, 'Oh yeah, another parole scam.' But checking my file, they saw that parole had been refused six months ago. I was already free, and everyone could see it.

Three days into my new life, I woke once again with something going on in my cell. A song woke me up. It was such a beautiful song that it caused me to snuggle down into my pillow, like a child under the loving stroke of a parent at night in bed. I started to stir from a deep slumber as the song invaded my heart and mind. My words are inadequate to explain it. I started to think, 'What is that wonderful noise, or sound, or song?' I could make no sense of it. It was gloriously simple. Two words, repeated three times: 'Sanctify him; sanctify him; sanctify him' – and then it evaporated.

As it lifted from me, or from my cell, or whatever was going on, I sat up to try and grasp it, to try and take ownership of it. As soon as it left, I could not re-create it. It was wonderful, yet gone. I sat still. The wonderful peace within my heart was still there, like a river flowing deep and slow. Underneath all the trappings and noisy hostility of prison life, and the impending release, and the following homelessness, there was a peace that transcends *all* understanding, unaffected by it all.

I started to entertain the word 'sanctify'. Not a word greatly used in my context. I said it to myself over and over – 'sanctify'. I felt like I almost knew what it meant, but just fell short of a tangible explanation. It was no real problem, though, because I had met the Lord Jesus. There I sat on my prison bed, trying to process all that had happened to me, and trying to make sense of this Jesus Christ making himself known to me, and now trying to piece together why there should be a song in my cell. And in the midst of it all, I had totally lost any and all desire to use drugs.

My whole desire system had been affected by my conversion to Christ. It was not that I had made a new decision to stop taking drugs; I had simply lost the inner urge to find and use drugs, and to repeat that destructive cycle. I had not stopped; God had removed the desire. Eventually, when the day started to break, and the birds started to sing to me, I ran down to Steve's cell and stood at the foot of his bed. I twisted his big toe. One has to be careful doing this sort of thing in prison. One can end up severely beaten!

Steve sat up with an astonished look in one eye, and the other would not quite open. He thought something was wrong. I asked him, 'What does "sanctify" mean?'

He sort of grunted something. I repeated my question. There followed a long silence and then an intake of breath, and he said, 'It means to set apart and purify.'

I walked away from Steve's cell that beautiful June morning, and I knew from deep within me that Jesus Christ was on my case and had begun the process of cleaning me up for his glory. I did not need anyone to tell me this, and I did not seek out anyone to confirm it. I knew that the Lord was at work in me. I inwardly seized Jesus and felt an enormous eruption of excitement at the potential for rescuing souls from the devil's grasp. I saw the truth that Jesus had been with me right throughout my dark life. He was there every step of the way. Right through the dark and dirty valley of sin and shame, Jesus kept me alive for such a time as this. I sat on my bed and looked at my life as one might look along the Grand Canyon. It was deep, long and frightening. I then looked to Jesus in my heart and said in absolute sincerity, 'Lord, I want to go back in. There are people in there dying without knowledge of your wonder.'

A prison officer was walking towards me one morning and I simply said to him, 'Good morning, boss.' He stopped and looked at me for a few moments and then in a really friendly tone replied, 'Good morning, Garnett.' I believe he not only saw a difference in my smiling face – he heard a difference in my voice, because I truly desired that he should have a 'good morning'. This was going to take a lot of getting used to, for everyone.

The lifer I was handcuffed to on my way to The Verne stopped me outside the chapel in that first week of my conversion. He and another lifer asked me to approach the chaplain and request a book from him. I was more than willing to agree.

I went into the chaplain's office and asked him for the book. He passed it to me, but kept hold of the book. He then questioned me, with what I thought was a cynical tone, about my experience that week: 'So what happened to you, then?'

If I had not met the Lord, his questioning would surely have birthed deep doubts in me. When he questioned me, I then remembered that he was actually in the service on the night I was saved, and I caught his eye then too. As I got out of the rubbish bin, it flashed through my mind that he was resentful towards me. I actually thought he was jealous of me, but dismissed this as my arrogance. I left his office feeling saddened and confused.

The two lifers did not look at the book; they were more interested in me. One of them asked, 'What's wrong?'

My thumb pointed over my shoulder to the chapel and I had to say, 'He is.'

They both changed towards me and said, 'You've been converted by the Spirit of God.' They then explained that the chaplain was suspected of being unconverted and the book thing was to test me.

We took the unconverted chaplain issue to prayer. I saw him five years later when he visited Bible college, and he was alive with Jesus.

New life

I had visited sixteen prisons during that sentence. The process of prison transfer is a process of degradation. Being stripped and searched where the sun fails to shine, pulled and pushed, talked at like an animal, and shifted around without identity or opinion. It had all reduced me to an internal state of nothingness. No identity and no hope, and yet it had to be that way for me. My circumstances crushed me and forced me to the feet of

God. He then gave me new life with identity, reason, purpose, hope and glory. Not only could I now look towards my release; I had the inward knowledge that it was not the prison system releasing me. Jesus had set me free. I started to think that if this continued, they were going to be releasing a free man! None of it made sense, yet it all made perfect sense.

My prayer life was tearful and passionate during this time. I spent the first two weeks confessing and rejoicing that he had set me free. My internal state was now a constant meditation on God – his character, his mercy, the nails, the cross, the blood, truth, freedom, joy, hope, peace. My heart simply flicked from one of his attributes to another. I was holding conversations with guys around me, but the wonders of Jesus never subsided.

It regularly came to mind that I had less than six months to serve. Towards the end of June 1993 I wrote to my dad. I had not heard from anyone in over sixteen months, and the sound of their disowning me still rang loudly in my heart. I wrote and I simply said, 'If you could see your way clear to visiting me, I would love to talk to you.' I sent him a visiting chit with the letter. Dad was sitting opposite me in the visiting room within three days. It was lovely to see this giant of a man again. We simply sat and stared at each other.

I broke the silence with, 'Dad, I have become a Christian.'

He leaned forward to hear me again and said, 'Sorry, son, I thought you said you'd become a Christian then.'

I knew it was too much for him because of our Catholic background. I tried another route. 'Dad, I have been born again, and I was baptized.'

There was a flash of apprehension on his face and he nervously asked, 'Have you kept the same name?'

I told him I was 'Garnett through and through', and gratefully proud to be his son and Mum's son and Alan and Linda's brother; but now Jesus Christ had saved me and my life belonged to him.

We both sat back and totally relaxed. We held hands. We got tearful. We hugged. From that time Dad sent me books, money, letters, tapes; he visited me and each time he did, he held my head and looked deep into my eyes. He regularly did this as his way of seeing my mum in my brown eyes. But now he was confused by what he saw. He saw Jesus in me.

I grew more and more aware of not having anywhere to live on my release. My prayers were along these lines: 'Lord, I know you hold the future. I need you to tell me where you want me on my release.' Each morning I got before him and asked, 'Lord, where do you want me?' One morning I sat before the Lord and gratefully declared, 'Lord, if you desire me homeless, I will declare your name amongst the homeless. If you desire that I go to cardboard city, Lord, to those meandering in isolation, I will gratefully go.' My heart was genuinely ready and grateful for such an honoured position. I had a Saviour who would walk with me and talk with me. He knew all about my being the Cultural Reject; he, too, was rejected by his own. He knew all about how the loneliness tried to crush me in solitary confinement; he, too, was very nearly crushed in isolation, so much so that angels ministered to him (Matt. 4:11).

Therefore I offered myself for cardboard city, with relish. I said this prayer with fervour and tears in my early-morning time with Jesus. I then got up to wash and shave. During my shave, I stared at my eyes and thought of the change I could see. I then thought of the prayer I had just said. I then sat back on my bed, and in a very child-like manner I simply said, 'Lord, if it is all right with you, I would prefer not to go to cardboard city.' Heaven smiled back at me.

It was in one of these deep and meaningful quiet times that the Lord gave me a startling revelation about myself. I was seeking his desire for when I got out. 'Where do you want me and what do you want me to do, Lord?' Within my heart, I felt and I knew that the Lord's will for me would be to 'do nothing for two years'. Of course, I dismissed this as totally ridiculous. Two years? I was raring to go now!

Then on a visit from Dad, he asked me what my plans were on my release. I saw he was nervous because I had ripped them all off so many times. He had the fear of me wanting to go and live with him and his wife. Their trust was severely damaged. I thought about the question, and answered, 'I am going to write to Nelson House in Stroud, and ask them if they would consider taking me back to try again.' This answer was like a revelation even to me, but as soon as I had said it, I knew that the Lord wanted me to return in humility, make amends with the people I had hurt, and try again. I also knew that he wanted me to 'do nothing for two years'. I did not try to explain the two-year thing; that was between God and myself at that point. Dad took my face in his hands and with tears in his eyes declared, 'That's my boy.' In a prison visiting room this sort of thing would have normally embarrassed me, but not now. No more. I was his boy and I was no longer enslaved by ego. I'd missed this man like words could not describe.

I wrote to Nelson House and applied for re-entry. They sent me a condition that I attend a therapy group being run in another prison in Surrey up until my release. This style of therapy, similar to the clinic I had been in, was a prerequisite for residence at Nelson House. I then applied for yet another prison transfer.

The wing officer looked at my file and the fact that I had been transferred sixteen times already, and he laughed at me. He asked me if I thought I was on a milk round. I smiled back at him, made my application and left his office.

Once again, within five hours, I was stood before a puzzled prison officer. He said, 'Who do you know?' I was formulating a gospel message response when he continued, 'Your name is on the list to be transferred next week.'

I went back to my cell and lay on my bed. In my heart I looked to the Lord and had to say, 'Lord, just take it easy with the grace; slow down a bit; I'm not sure I can handle it.' Heaven smiled back at me again. In my heart I was also aware that I had been given a wonderful window of gospel opportunity when the officer said, 'Who do you know?' – and I missed it. I knew that if that guy went to eternal hell, his blood would be on my hands. The severity of not knowing Jesus dawned clearer and clearer by the day for me, and a burning question haunted me: 'How can I keep this to myself?' My prayer life intensified.

I arrived at HMP Downview, onto the Addicted Prisoners' Trust Programme, in late August 1993. I had four months of group and one-to-one therapy to negotiate, and it was time to make my stand for Jesus. I had been handcuffed to a guy claiming to have a chunk of weed inside him, and 'we' would get stoned as soon as 'we' arrived at Downview.

I saw him the next day. He was rolling a joint by the gym. I went and stood with him. He started to smoke the joint and comment on the quality of the weed. He passed the joint to me and I said, 'No thanks, I don't need it.'

Up until this point, since my conversion, I had smoked several joints of weed. I had smoked it, but it did not get me stoned. I had smoked with the circle of guys I was in with at The Verne. In fact, since my conversion, they went out of their way to smoke in my cell. I smoked, but nothing happened to me. The day before I left The Verne, these guys produced ten litres of home-brewed booze and a chunk of weed. I sat in with them until they were all stoned and drunk, but I remained stone-cold straight and sober, and they all knew it. It was difficult for me to grasp that even smoking weed was over, but equally difficult for me to say no to the guys who had become my party hosts.

The freedom I had been given now seemed to intensify. I was set free at another level, and I walked away from the drug scene at that point. I was still smoking cigarettes, though. But that didn't bother me, because it was not me who stopped my drug use. The Lord Jesus had set me free. So when he removed the tobacco addiction, I would stop smoking too. I was, however, able to give half of my weekly tobacco allowance away to strugglers around me. I accepted that there was no point in judging them, because unless Jesus did a work in them, I had no right to 'expect better' from them. I have no doubt in my heart that Jesus had released me from the nicotine addiction, though, because I no longer enjoyed the taste or the smell of the smoke. I was actually afraid of not smoking. I had always enjoyed a cigarette; it had a calming effect on me. I could not grasp that I no longer needed them. The desire had been removed, but the courage to change the behaviour pattern was missing.

The therapy group consisted of approximately ten other guys. In that group I came face to face with heavy gangsters who had fallen prey to heroin. They were aggressive and very confrontational. I was clean from narcotics. I started to accumulate 'clean-time'. I can remember, as if it was this morning, the first time I reached seven days clean. I was actually clean, in prison! I had a thousand justifications for smoking weed, and yet there I was, seven days clean. I had no inclination to boast at all. I had not done it – Jesus had. I was amazed that my life could function 'clean'. In-group I became the butt of some very venomous sarcasm, and the whisper- ing and laughing plucked at the chords of shame in me which had been instilled in the classroom over twenty- five years earlier when everyone around me pointed and laughed at me. The shame was still deep, but I knew I could now take hold of it and take it to my Lord. Everything the devil threw at me, I took to God, and he did some wonderful healing work in me, once again, among the unbelievers.

Everyone else in the group was still using weed, and my being clean threatened every one of them. They each tried to get me to smoke with them, and they collect- ively rejected me for being 'teacher's pet'. They attacked me verbally every day in-group. I just sat and took it, acknowledging the fear and the injustice of their cruelty, trusting God to see me through. It was very hard to express these fears and struggles, but every time I did, I grew. It was hard, because every time I said, 'I feel hurt by your cruelty,' it was like a red rag to a bull. I was bombarded with abuse and ridicule, but slowly I grew in inner maturity and in the handling of these situations. I started to recognize how the pain of the verbal ridicule never lasted if I answered with the truth of the pain.

Sometimes, though, some things were said and the pain would not go away as easily. I would even wake up with the pain the next day. I then started to see that, in amongst the 'abuse', there was very often some truth about me that I would have to get before God in prayer about. I was unknowingly developing discernment between good and bad abuse. Some things were said to harm me, which was bad abuse. Others things were said and they hurt, but it was healthy abuse. The truth often hurt, but it never caused any harm. Slander and sarcasm is designed to destroy.

Looking to God's Word for guidance, I found this text in Hebrews: 'Solid food belongs to those who are of full age, that is, those who by reason of use have their senses exercised to discern both good and evil' (Heb. 5:14 NKJV). I realized that good advice does not necessarily mean it has to be 'good sounding'. It may hurt, but the content is nourishing if digested, like most medicines. Spiritual medicines, such as constructive criticism, don't taste like honey!

Slowly, over the next three months, I could feel myself growing. This was confirmed when each group member came to my cell to apologize and express respect, some even asking me to pray for them. I was puzzled as to why I had to endure such hostility and was starting to feel very sorry for myself. I was of the opinion that this group needed me more than I needed it, and although I sat in the therapeutic group circle, I was not actually a part of the group. I knew that I had to stay focused on God and keep turning to him at every available quiet moment, and he would sustain me, and attract them to himself in his way. During the darkest hour of the persecutions at Downview, I sat on my bed in the early hours of the morning, preparing for another day of it. Turning to God's Word, my attention was caught by Jeremiah 15:16–21 (NASB):

> I have been called by Your name
> O Lord God of hosts.
> I did not sit in the circle of merrymakers,
> Not did I exult.

Because of Your hand upon me I sat alone,
For You filled me with indignation.
Why has my pain been perpetual
And my wound incurable, refusing to be healed?
Will You indeed be to me like a deceptive stream
With water that is unreliable?
Therefore, thus says the Lord,
'If you return, then I will restore you –
Before Me you will stand.
And if you extract the precious from the worthless,
You will become My spokesman.
They for their part may turn to you,
But as for you, you must not turn to them.
Then I will make you to this people
A fortified wall of bronze;
And though they fight against you
They will not prevail over you;
For I am with you to save you
And deliver you,' declares the Lord.
'So I will deliver you from the hand of the wicked,
And I will redeem you from the grasp of the violent.'

I actually felt sorry for these guys, because they had no idea who this God was who they were up against. There was one guy who was ruthless in his mockery of Jesus. He died of an overdose one week after his release. My personal counsellor, a Kiwi guy called Eddie, actually ended up receiving my counsel about 'the peace that transcends all understanding'. He said, 'I am jealous of the quality of spirituality you have.'

My clean time grew, and my personal time with Jesus went from depth to depth. I was in a single cell, on a section of the jail dominated by Yardies (Jamaican gangsters). I was one of three white guys on that section of the prison. Next to me, on one side was a heroin and dope dealer, and on the other there was an ex-IRA terrorist. The dope deal-er had nothing to do with the therapy group; the terrorist was very heavily into heroin and was a dominant member of the group. One night, I was chatting to the terrorist. A hot-water pipe ran through the length of the wing. If one wrapped a towel around the pipe and placed one's head side-on to it, we could see each other and chat away.

I asked John[10] why he was so hostile towards God. His response blew me away. He said, 'Colin, I was chased out of Ireland by the IRA. I was running amok. I got such a high from killing that I used to kill IRA members. Then I went on revenge killings, killing two for every one of us. One night they [the IRA] came for me, but I escaped.' I wrote a prayer out on some toilet roll and slid it through the wall to him. John went quiet for twenty minutes or so, until I heard him quietly weeping. He wept for the rest of the time I was awake. The dope deal-er on the other side got involved and ended up offering me some free weed. I quietly declined, telling him I had no need of it. The silence from his cell was strangely deafening. I knew the Lord was revealing himself to some very heavy criminals around me. I had a deep, burning desire to help these guys, because I knew that, just like I had been only five months earlier, they were heading in the wrong direction.

Love of the Word

My hunger for God's Word was insatiable. I had two or three Bibles opened all the time. I was comparing texts in different translations, and writing notes. I had notes all over my cell, piles of them on different verses and translations. One morning at approximately 4 a.m. I was awake and singing praises to God. I had been sent a

Walkman by my dad and a worship tape by Irene Long. I was tearfully worshipping the Lord.

I heard the night officer on his rounds, entering our wing. I heard him as he worked his way from cell to cell doing the nightly count. As he came to my cell, he paused for ten or fifteen seconds and watched me as I worshipped the true and living God. I was singing loud enough to be heard, but not loud enough to disturb. The night officer walked away from my cell and a few moments later he returned. He simply stood and watched me in worship. The prison officers were being reached too.

Knowing that this guy could be from among the ranks of the doomed, I became very aware of what I was singing, and the depth of theology within the words. Fortunately I was singing, 'You laid aside your majesty', and I felt secure that it had attractive truth within it. I seemed to have an awareness of the potential damage Satan could cause within mankind with counterfeit spirituality.

It was during one of these worship sessions that I broke down on my bed and wept before God, 'Lord, I want to take this testimony right into the enemy's backyard.' I was haunted by the thoughts of all the men and women I had known who had died from addiction, and of all those in the rehabs and treatment centres who were desperately wanting to be clean, but who were seeking in the wrong directions.

Heaven smiled back at me. Not only was I already in the enemy's backyard, I had to learn how my internal sense of security and the joy within my heart had blinded me to the darkness around me. The only mentoring I had received thus far had been from the lifer. The insight I felt was quite frightening. I joined a Bible study group run by the chaplain. Following one session, frustrated by our debate about conversion, he asked, 'So where does that leave me?' I lacked the courage to tell him he was lost forever without being born again into Christ, because he was wearing a dog collar and I was wearing stripes!

The Christians visiting from outside were astounded by what was taking place in my life. I was approached by one of them and asked if there was anything I needed. It was time for some humility on my part. I was in need of shoes. The training shoes I went into this sentence with were pretty much falling off my feet. I struggled to ask. I felt pride and shame all at the same time. I had to ask myself, 'If this person was my brother and he was in need, would I not want to help him?' Off the back of this I assured myself that I was now actually his brother in Christ, and so I pointed him to my need.

Within a week I was walking around the jail in a new pair of training shoes. It was an awesome time for me. I had something new, and there was no desire within me to sell them for drugs. I felt a true sense of appreciation. They weren't the top brand name, which bothered me – so there was an image issue that needed to be addressed before God. I went on to learn that as I arrived at a place of being truly grateful, the image problem lost its power over me, and brand names were no longer an issue. It is not *what* I wear – it is *why*.

I was silently intrigued by the fact that I was getting into bed at night and falling straight to sleep. Every night since my conversion I had slept straight through without disturbance. I had been in the 'only three months to go' place several times before, and I knew that it was gate-fever time. I should have been tossing and turning the night away, planning my future, where I will go, where I won't go, what job I will get, and how different life will be this time out. It all starts to churn through the imagination at approximately three months left to do. I was actually waiting for the gate fever to take hold, but it simply did not kick in. Each day was a day in the company of Jesus, and each night was peaceful and calm, all without drugs. My mind regularly drifted forward to my release date, but only in wondering if I would sleep the night before my release.

Two days before my release, the Rehabilitation of Prisoners Trust awarded me their Certificate of Completion, as I came to the end of their prison treatment programme. Jesus was within me at this stage, but due to the stress of being drug free in prison, and my impending drug-free release, my weight was down to 59 kilograms (I was 15 kilos underweight). God did not remove these stresses; he empowered me to handle them, and at the end of the day, any 'normal' person would be underweight in the same set of circumstances. I was 'normal'.

My clean time grew, as did the resentment towards me in those group sessions. It was a terrible time of emotional bullying and suffering, but now I was suffering for belonging to Jesus, and that I could live with. It was healthy suffering. I was asked by one of the group if I would urinate into a container for him so that he would get through the random tests we were subjected to as part of the therapy. I declined, but another guy claiming clean time said he would do it. I knew in my heart that this guy was only drug free, as opposed to 'clean'. The drugs were absent, but the behaviour remained the same. As it turned out, we all had to give urine samples, and these two characters went through the urine-by-deception routine, and they both tested positive. It was the funniest thing: when challenged as to 'Why did you tell me you were clean?', the other guy just shrugged and said, 'I didn't tell you I was clean; I told you I would piss in your container.'

It was good to be free. I was so glad that I had been given the opportunity to bin the other life. I grew in gratitude that Jesus had set me free from this worldly calibre of relationship. But it was the only calibre of relationship I had ever known, so I knew I was going to struggle in the relationship area.

I reached my release date six months clean. The night before I got out, sure enough, I got into bed and slept like a log right through the night. I was free indeed. I was released the next morning and given my release grant of £52. Two other guys were released the same day, and I felt a deep sense of compassion for both of them. They had plans to conquer the world and their addiction 'this time out'. I'd been at that point five times before, and I knew they still had lots of jail left in them.

They released a free man.

Chapter 7

The Bondages of Freedom

I had money in my pocket for the first time in two years. It was only £52, but it felt like a mountain of money to me. It was two days before Christmas. I felt a distinct pull towards Manchester for a very brief moment, but knew I would not fit in up there any longer, and on the platform at the railway station, I inwardly underwent a grieving type of experience. I could see the train bound for Manchester and I knew I could be with Hayley within three hours if I chose. The pull was almost physical.

I turned to the Lord in my heart and said something along the lines of 'Lord, you know exactly what is going on in me right now. I am going to leave that chapter of my life in your care, and turn my back on it all.' With that, I decided to board a train heading in the opposite direction. My freedom and peace went to a new level.

I posted £35 to Hayley for her Christmas box, bought myself a chocolate bar and a Coke, and caught the train to the Cotswolds. I had actually browsed through a few shops first, but saw nothing that I wanted. I had everything I needed. A train ticket to new relationships and all the help I would need, and Jesus as Saviour. I gave my daughter her first honest Christmas gift. It was not stolen or bought with stolen money, and I felt an inner peace about the whole future.

On the train I saw humanity in its hopelessness, and a burden to cast Jesus' light started to grow at a rapid rate within me, but I could not escape the Lord's two-year time-out period. I did not understand it, but I now knew that there were many things beyond my understanding that I simply had to go with. The train ride from London to Stroud took me through some of England's finest countryside. It was winter and the fields were white with frost. I was in absolute awe at how God looks after the land, suddenly knowing that the frost was just as important as the sunshine for the farmers and the crops. I saw God everywhere – even in the suffering people in whom he was working to fulfil his purpose, just as he had in my life.

I arrived at Nelson House by midday. The moment I met the lady who ran Nelson House, she stepped back and said, 'Your eyes have changed.'

I said, 'That's Jesus.'

Mary had seen me at my worst on my last visit to Nelson House, and she knew all too well what I used to be like.

On my previous visit, I was told that it was forbidden to leave the house alone for the first two weeks, but within two hours I had gone out to the shop alone. I reasoned that I had been in jail three months, and primary treatment for three months. I needed a break from being escorted everywhere, and I simply had to have some stationery in order to write to my daughter. At the shop I found I was short of cash. I was buying a pen, a pad, envelopes and a stamp. I slid the pen up my sleeve and paid for the rest. I was breaking the rules of the house and still thieving as a matter of routine, and actually using the name of Hayley and my 'imagined' relationship with her as a means of justification. I made it sound like I had a wonderful relationship with Hayley, and in many ways I did, but on the whole it was stained by crime and disruption and was very damaging.

This second time at Nelson, though, not only did I fall in line with house expectations; I actually wanted to. I had a new kind of battle taking place within me about being at Nelson House this time, but I made a conscious decision to yield to their regime. My confusion was: 'I now know Jesus as my guide and counsellor. He is my all-in-all. Why do I need to attend a secular rehab home if I am now confessing Jesus as Lord?' I did not allow this argument any expression. I simply waited, knowing that the Lord would reveal to me his wisdom in his time.

I enjoyed waking up early each morning and sitting with the Lord, listening to the birds singing and watching the winter. It was awesome. My restriction period passed quite quickly and I ventured out alone for the first time. I walked by the canal and talked to the Lord about where I was and why. I ended up outside the shop where I had stolen the pen. I went into the shop and bought myself some chocolate. I also bought the same sort of pen as the one I had stolen months before. After paying for this one, I returned it to the shelf. Life started to make sense. I left that shop knowing that I was 'approved of God'. I knew his smile upon my life. I felt truly close to Jesus himself.

On a high, I decided to travel into Stroud by bus. I had forgotten to get change for the bus ride and only had a £5 note. When I got onto the bus I approached the driver with my money in hand, and suddenly my confidence just drained out of me. I did not know how to communicate with this guy. I suddenly felt terribly vulnerable.

I heard myself say: 'Is this bus going to Stroud?'

The driver came back with an 'ask a stupid question, get a stupid answer' tone and said: 'What does it say on the front?'

I nearly exploded. In my heart I wanted to slam his head into the ticket machine and drag him off the bus. I actually lost my breath with the surge of energy in me towards this guy.

I gave him the note and said nothing more. I sat on that bus and knew in my heart that although the Lord Jesus had saved me out of the world for himself in an instant, getting the world out of me was going to be a long process. I had actually felt vulnerable in this, the simplest of life's situations, and reacted with aggression. A new feeling, same old response.

I instantly knew that I would hereafter have to watch myself. As soon as I started to feel good about my Christianity, I was susceptible to the old nature rising up in me, and sin was crouching at the door, desiring me.

It also became a reality for me that there was a lot of 'making right' to do in my life, particularly in the everyday relational issues, and that would take time. People had heard my apologies year after year; now it was time for Colin to actually change and let the people see my sincerity. Nelson House had many guidelines and expectations. One of them was regular attendance at Narcotics and/or Alcoholics Anonymous meetings. I had attended NA for several years at this point, but never quite managed to get clean. Now I was clean and free in Christ, but it was now slowly dawning on me that these groups had many diamonds and pearls of wisdom essential for my context of recovery and reintegration into mainstream society. I was deeply in love with Jesus Christ, and everything belonged to him. I knew he would never abandon me, even if I were making a mistake going to the world for guidance.

NA had this thing about not flying deity-specific flags in their meetings. Jesus was not to be proclaimed as Saviour, because it was 'each to his own'. They offered 'the god of your own understanding', and each individual brought in their own interpretation of who or what God was. I threw myself into the NA meetings and saturated myself in 'recovery' literature. The more I attended these meetings, and the more I shared one-to-one fellowship with NA members, the more frustrated I became.

I was identifying myself at meetings, five and six times a week as: 'I'm Colin, I'm an addict.' Every time I said this I had an inner belief that I was in the midst of believing a lie. I was actually creating an identity that would make sense of all the years of active destruction behind me. I then started to see that people were not actually creating a 'god of their own understanding'; they were creating a 'self' of their own understanding. It was just another version of the problem – a cleaner, safer version; but it was still a case of 'following the crowd, just to fit in'.

A role model

At Nelson House one afternoon I got a phone call. A guy on the other end of the line asked me if I would like to 'share fellowship at their church this Sunday'. From deep within me I knew that this guy was a part of the answer to my prayers and that my Christian needs were about to be met. He said, 'We are a small charismatic fellowship and this Sunday is a fellowship lunch. Do you fancy coming along?' I agreed to join them and as I replaced the receiver to its cradle, my heart started to pound within me, because I knew the Lord was sending someone to guide me into the next chapter of my life.

That Sunday morning I was up and ready by 7.00 a.m. He had arranged to collect me at 9:30. I sat looking out of the window like a little boy looking for

Santa Claus. It was really weird. I was only going to church, for heaven's sake – what was there to be excited about? At 9:30, a guy knocked at the door of Nelson House. As I met him he stretched out his hand and smiled straight into my eyes and simply said, 'Hi, I'm Andy Morris.'

That was pretty much the sum total of this guy's introduction, but something happened inside of me that I would never be able to explain. I just totally relaxed around this guy. He was of a similar height to me, and a similar age. In fact, as it turned out, Andy was born a matter of hours before me. Andy: 4 February 1959. Me: 5 February 1959. My initial thoughts were: 'The Lord has sent me a role model.' I had a lot of street and prison image to get out of my system, and I knew it. What I did not know, though, was how I would fill the void left by what had to be removed. In Andy Morris I instantly saw enviable godly characteristics more than worthy of emulation. I saw Jesus in Andy and felt a healthy envy of him. I knew I would be spending time with this guy in the coming months.

Within ten minutes of leaving Nelson House that morning, we had arrived at Minchinhampton Christian Fellowship. It was a social-club-type building, used by the local youth for a Friday night youth club. In my eyes, we were lost in the outback of the UK. It was typical English country life, but for some strange reason I felt at home. People came and greeted me. They were relaxed and wearing bright colours. Children ran around and made children's noises. People hugged each other, and there were cakes and biscuits, soft drinks and more cakes. It was totally revolutionary to my mind-set. I did not know church could be like this.

I caught people looking at my tattoos from time to time and then smiling with embarrassment, not knowing what to make of me. In this hidden little fellowship in the countryside, consisting of school-teachers and shop-owners, the Lord had placed me – a heavily tattooed ex-intravenous drug addict of seventeen years, who had just been released from a brutal lifestyle and prison, and yet was now fired up for God. This was going to be interesting, to say the least! I sat with Andy and his lovely family, and simply melted into Minchinhampton Christian Fellowship.

My second week at Minch included going to Andy's parents for lunch, where we all sat around a fully laid-out table as a family to eat. It was the weirdest thing for me to sit in a quiet family environment and eat. I felt like a caveman among royalty, but I caught my first glimpse of 'family life' as the posh people live it.

I grew up with my plate of food on my knee in front of the telly, feeling like I had to finish first or get robbed by my older siblings. Now it was all polite and proper. Inside I was as nervous as hell, and yet laughing away to myself at my ignorance. I had to watch which knife to use and remember not to belch out loud as a sign of pleasure. I wanted to belch, simply to see what the reaction would be, but I resisted.

The Morris family were, and still are, the most beautiful people I know, and I love them dearly. I could see that they were going out of their way to accommodate me and they collectively contributed to my maturity, even in ways that they will never know. It sounds like a far cry from a prison cell and heroin addiction, particularly if you are trapped in that cycle as you read. But in actual fact, for me it was just one prayer away, and it can be for you too.

The elders of the church all went out of their way to help me settle into my new life, and I would not be where I am now if it were not for their efforts and grace. They simply loved me.

Then one Sunday morning the strangest thing happened. As I was sitting listening to the message, I had a strange sense that someone was watching me. To my left I found a little boy aged eighteen months or so. He simply stood and stared at me. I felt the only natural thing to do was offer my open hands for him to climb onto my knee if he so wished. He held my eye contact with a very slight hint of a smile, like he almost recognized me. Then he climbed onto my knee and fell sound asleep.

I felt like I had stolen him, and looked round to find his family. They were all sitting two rows behind me, and were smiling unconditionally at me. His mum and dad just shrugged and gestured for me to let him sleep.

The majority of the people in the church were quite rightly cautious of me, but this little man was totally relaxed with me. When he started to stir, I felt a sense of panic welling up in me. He would be expecting to be fed, and I was simply not equipped! He would want to see his mum, but when he saw me he would surely panic.

When he awoke, he sat up and got his bearings for a moment and then turned to look at me. He looked straight into my eyes. We held eye-to-eye contact for another beautiful moment, and then he smiled and went straight back to sleep. I cruised past the point of no return at that moment and knew that it was time for me to fit in.

I went back to Nelson House that afternoon, and sat in silent awe at how God got his heartbeat across. I was invited back to the little man's home the following week for lunch, and fell safely in love with his whole family – Peter, Vanessa, Joshua, Jordan, Amy and Laura Record. It was an amazing thing to sit in among 'normal' folk and actually feel a sense of belonging. The more they loved me, the easier it became for me to allow my mask to drop.

The 34-year-old teenager

But then the weirdest thing started to happen in me. Remember that I had vanished into the behavioural patterns rooted in addiction decades earlier. I had lost the ability to express my feelings in an adequate manner, and so adopted a way of self-governing my emotional realm. I was either funny or angry, with very little in between. So now, as I started to relax in this new life, the suppressed emotions started to surface. I was 34 years old, feeling inferior and unsafe with adults, and strangely attracted to teenagers. Not in any sexual sense. It was just an inner safety that I felt around the younger generation. I mentioned it to some of the guys around me and they hinted that it could be a call to youth work. I knew that it was not. I knew that I had to be secure with adults before I could ever lead the youth anywhere. In his mercy God gave me an awareness of what was happening to me, and the two-year time-out period started to make some sort of sense.

I also started getting in touch with a very deep desire to be with a woman. I would sit in group sessions at Nelson, and find myself inwardly yearning to be in some sort of contact with a woman. No one specific woman, just some feminine input. I had been in an all-male, macho environment for so long that the feminine felt really attractive to me. I was afraid of my feelings by this stage and started to keep them to myself again.

Once a wdeek I went to the cell group that gathered at Andy's home, and together we shared fellowship and testimonies. I grew in love and respect for Andy and his family. I learned from Andy, even when he did not know I was watching him. Each week I gave testimony of people whom I had seen come to the Lord through my personal witness to them. I could not grasp how anyone could go through a day without talking to a lost soul about this Jesus.

I was once asked, 'Why do you think you lead so many to the Lord?'

I could only respond by saying, 'Because that is exactly how I expect it to be and nothing less will do. The Lord Jesus Christ has redeemed my very soul from the clutches of Lucifer himself, and liberated me from the daily nightmare of addiction into the glorious freedom of his light and truth.'

I started going up to the top of one of the valleys very early in the mornings to sing to the King – just simply for that sole purpose. It was a debt of love from a grateful heart. I would shout out 'Thank you, Jesus!' and sing and dance for the Lord himself. It was awesome.

Minchinhampton Christian Fellowship carried me though many turbulent times in my first two years as a Christian, and many souls have been found and converted as a result of their mentorship, grace and patience with me.

After six months at Nelson House, I started to feel a pull towards leaving. Every week in the Peer Evaluation Group, I got the same feedback from the whole house: 'Keep on doing what you are doing.' But in my heart I knew that I was starting to backslide.

I had allowed myself to become emotionally involved with one of the female residents, and we were both starting to make it sound like it was God's plan for us. I started getting involved in secret meetings with this lady, and even though nothing physical was taking place between us, flirting with the idea was under way.

I did not have any means of protecting myself from this emotional involvement, and it became apparent that I not only had a lot to learn, I also had a great deal to unlearn. I had no skills in avoiding this kind of situation, and it actually felt like I was sliding down the side of a wet embankment into a whole new valley of struggle.

But the Lord helped me get my life back in line with his heartbeat and I started to move on. I went from Nelson House to sharing a house with a lady who had been in NA for over ten years. I occupied the top of the house, she had the bottom and we shared the kitchen. She had no name for her god. Whenever she hit hard times and struggles, she made reference to her 'higher power', but would not give it a name. It was impersonal.

Linda

I answered the door one day and almost fell through the floor to see my brother Alan standing there. Something was terribly wrong. There was a pregnant silence between us until he stepped inside and said, 'It's Lin. She has cancer.'

I simply asked, 'Is she going to die?'

To which he took me in his arms and said, 'Not necessarily.'

I packed a bag and we were heading south towards Dad's place within thirty minues.

Dad knew something was wrong as soon as he saw Alan and I turn up at his home on the south coast. He met each of us eye-to-eye and simply asked us 'Who?' We sat him down and explained that Lin had cancer. It was of the most severe kind, at the entrance of her stomach, and there was a very low success rate for this type of operation.

Dad instantly adopted the stiff-upper-lip, never-say-die attitude, but I expressed my anger and fear of losing my sister at such an early age. With that, it seemed that everyone got in touch with the same feelings, and we were able then to rally round each other in a time of grief.

At Linda's request, we did not all gather by her beside. I returned to Stroud, Dad stayed where he was and Alan returned home. We just sat and waited. I got before my Lord and placed my sister into his hands.

I wrote Linda a letter and tried to reach her in her terrible state of desperation. I spoke of the desperation I had regularly felt when trapped in addiction, and of the inner knowledge that no one really understood how I truly felt. I then said that in her loneliest and most desperate of moments, Jesus would understand and respond if she called to him.

That was in 1994. Today, in 2008, I speak to my sister very regularly. She is now fully fit and working in health-care herself, having come through with flying colours.

Returning to Stroud, things soon took another turn for my growth. After six months of sharing the house with the NA lady, I went down to the kitchen to find her sitting in the dark weeping. Before I had an opportunity to say anything, she started with, 'Colin, I feel like I'm dying. You have such life and consistency, but I cannot get out of this darkness!'

The opening was clear; I said to her, 'You're right, you are dying, and in your own choice of darkness.'

I told her about Jesus. That night, after ten years of self-generated recovery, she came face to face with the truth of who Jesus is.

Moving on

The next morning I knew my mission at that address was complete and it was time for me to move on, and that day I moved out and into a little bed-sit of my own, and I just loved it. At night I would close my curtains and do stupid, child-like dancing for the Lord. Often I would weep whilst dancing in the presence of the King I loved. I set him a chair in the middle of the room and danced for him, before sitting on the floor at his feet and thanking him for saving me. I had failed him miserably, and used to take pleasure from being his enemy, and yet he still remained faithful.

I occupied that little flat for six more months. I had many non-Christian visitors, some of whom received Christ for forgiveness and salvation, while others took the truth away with them. I delivered the message with every ounce of passion within me – it was then between the sinner and God. I knew that God's Holy Spirit had to convict them of their sin.

I then heard of some new flats being built in a little village called Nailsworth. I got a good feeling about these flats as soon as I heard about them, and I felt that the Lord was waiting for me to ask him, and he would give me whatever my heart desired. I made visiting them my next venture. I had come from jail to Nelson House, then into shared accommodation, then into a single bed-sit of my own. I now just felt it was time to progress some more.

I visited the building-site that was to become new flats. I climbed over cement bags and upturned crates to get to the top floor. There were three flats on the top floor and I walked into the middle one. I just knew that this was going to be my next home. I took the number of the flat (7), and the phone number of the landlord, and rang him that day. I was invited to fill in application forms.

I agreed to fill them in, but said to the guy, 'I want number 7.'

He said, 'That's all good and well, but there is a waiting list that you will have to join first, and we have to assess your suitability.'

I said, 'Go ahead, but I want number 7.'

He said, 'Why number 7?'

I told him, 'Because 7 is God's number, and I belong to him.'

He came round to interview me at my bed-sit the next day, and it seemed that he actually struggled not to give me the keys to number 7. He kept justifying why I should not have this flat: 'There is a twelve-month waiting list. . . . You have to follow procedure. . . . There are forms you have to complete.'

I just sat there and prayed all over him. Then shaking his head in a type of disbelief, he gave me the keys to number 7.

One week later, I moved into my own little flat overlooking the village of Nailsworth in the Gloucestershire countryside. My dancing before God increased, as did the tears of gratitude. I was speaking to my family regularly by now, and during one conversation with my brother, I said, 'I would love a home of my own on the side of a valley,' and we both chuckled.

I had been out of prison almost two years, when I gave testimony at a healing meeting near Cirencester. Following my testimony, a Baptist minister approached me. He asked me if I knew Vic Jackopson. I said I had never heard of him. He then went on to tell me how Vic was an ex-villain who had founded Hope Now Ministry and how he was going to Ukraine in the summer to visit prisons out there. I knew without a shred of doubt right there and then that I was going to Ukraine with this Vic guy, whoever he was. The two-year period was up and God was remaining faithful to the conviction he had given me.

I went to Andy the next day and simply said, 'I'm going to Ukraine.' I wrote to Hope Now the same day, introducing myself with a seven-line testimony. I poured out my heart in those seven lines and expressed my frustrations in these words: 'There must be more to this church thing than setting out chairs week in, week out, and gathering in holy huddles.'

Within one week I had received a response from Vic himself saying, 'Ask your church for support, but if they cannot help, I will personally pay for you. You are coming to Ukraine.' God was about to open a new chapter in my life, and I knew with a deep excitement that this Jackopson character would be playing a significant role in my future. I thought that getting a passport might be a problem, but my application went without a hitch.

Chapter 8

Hope Now

Correspondence came through from Hope Now and I suddenly found myself in possession of an air ticket to Kiev. I stared at it for hours, and kept repeating to myself, 'I'm going to Ukraine to talk about Jesus.' There was a team of Hope Now supporters going on the trip and we were called to meet at Whitton Baptist Church in London, the night before we were due to fly out. At Whitton, when people started to arrive, I started to feel a welling up of excitement. I felt a real sense of purpose, and all my struggles and frustrations of the previous two years slid into insignificance.

When Vic arrived, I saw an immediate presence to him. I saw Jesus in his eyes, heard wisdom in his words, and a gentle authority in his tone. A man of God. He shook my hand and as we held eye-to-eye contact, we checked each other out, and knew within seconds that this was more than just fellowship – it was kindred-spirit affinity of character. I knew that this guy, with all his godliness, would fit in on any prison exercise yard. He was neither a victim nor a hunter; he was at peace and I loved him from the off. He spoke to me as an equal.

The whole team sat in a circle in the church hall and each member was asked to give a short testimony, saying who he or she was and where they were from. We had schoolteachers, child-minders, doctors, students, nurses, a few other folk and me. My heavily tattooed hand caught many an eye, and as I shared a very brief testimony, the room went from being quiet, to very quiet. But then Vic appointed me policeman over the baggage, and the irony brought an explosion of laughter.

Patricia

On the flight I found myself sitting next to a female member of the team, and she looked terribly nervous about me. I believed that if I had yelled 'Boo!' at her, she would have had the plane turn around for her to get off and go home where she would be safe. She came across as very polite, but ready to run at the first hint of any mischief. Once again, Vic helped melt the ice when he asked this lady and I to count the money out into thousands of dollars. We were suddenly sat with a pile of dollars between us, and she went from being a bag of nerves, to a wonderful sister in Christ with the best sense of humour I have ever come across. Patricia Jackopson-Hendy, Vic's sister-in-law, became my best friend before we touched tarmac in Kiev.

So much so that she was nagging me before we reached check-in at the airport. 'Come this way, carry this, go that way, nag, nag, nag, nag, nag.' I rejoiced in how God had given me such a trusting friend, which in turn told me that I could trust her. During the bus ride from the airport Trish, now totally relaxed, was chatting quite a lot. I waited for a pause and then jumped in with, 'Boy, can you talk!'

Trish, and several people sat closest to us, went into a kind of amazed silence. I looked her right in the eye and said to her, 'I'm betting you could talk a glass eye to sleep.' There was a slight lull, and then an almighty eruption of laughter. From that time on Trish and Roy, her husband, have been friends in the truest sense, who tell me exactly what I need to hear when I need it. I could only thank God for the blessing of this nervous lady feeling totally safe with me.

The Lord was constantly making his heart for me known to me through his children. I found that every time I was asked a question, people seemed to hang on every word I said. Very often some would jump in to prove me wrong or dismantle my theological views; but on the whole, I seemed to capture respect.

Prison 62

It was in Prison 62, Cherkassey, that I received my deepest blessing since climbing into the trash can two years previously. The prison was in a shocking state of decay, and the prisoners blended in very well. They were thick-skinned and as rough as they come. Something like 300 men packed into the tiny chapel, and we spent some time singing praises to God.

Following the worship, Vic took to the pulpit and opened God's Word. For the first time in my Christian life, I could honestly say that I was listening to God's Word, being unpacked by a man anointed and filled with God's Spirit. I was suddenly being scratched where I itched, theologically. It was like having a cold shower. I felt totally refreshed by biblical exposition.

I looked to Trish sitting next to me, and simply said to her, 'He is sitting in my seat.'

Trish was shocked and looked around to see if anyone had overheard. 'What do you mean?'

I shrugged my shoulders and simply said, 'I don't know what it means, but I know that this man is sitting in my seat.'

Trish said, 'You have to tell him.'

I avoided her idea. 'No way! If it is of God, let God tell him.'

At that point, I knew, without need of man's approval, that I had to get alongside this little giant of a man, and sit at his feet whenever I could for learning. I started to watch him closely.

Following his sermon, Vic turned to me and simply said, 'Colin, testify.' I simply took it in my stride, stood up and gave a twenty-minute testimony of God's liberating mercy. Everyone felt how God rested his hand upon that meeting, and no one moved or said a word throughout the sermon and then the testimony.

Vic took the pulpit again, and laid the truth before these men. We saw approximately 250 prisoners respond to an altar call for salvation.

The team members were astonished, and actually looked surprised. I closed my eyes and got myself before God as best I could. At the response of these men, I inwardly and sin-wardly felt a sense of self-satisfaction and righteousness, as if I had achieved something. I sat before God and simply opened my hands before him. Distorted motives are never very far from the surface. I received, however, a deep and blessed assurance within me, that the Lord Jesus himself had drawn and saved the majority of these men that day. The Word, carried by the Spirit, took souls into humility, and God then caused these weeping souls to be born again.

I was asked afterwards, 'Why do you think so many got saved?'

Without doubt I answered, 'Because it was exactly what we had expected.'

God remains faithful to his word that 'the Son of Man came to seek and save what was lost' (Luke 19:10). He does not save people because of me; he saves them despite me, and that's the essence of grace and mercy. If God had to wait until his messengers were pure to save others, we would all be doomed.

Back at the campsite that night, we sat in silent awe and prayed for God's new adopted sons in Prison 62. I kept my thoughts to myself, but the worship took on a new depth of sincerity and meaning for every one of us; we worshipped him in spirit and in truth. As we worshipped, I saw much spiritual light around me. Most of us wept quietly before we slowly filtered off to bed against a cacophony of Ukrainian night sounds. Several team members got their walk with God back in step, too, at that time. God has not finished with any of us.

As that 1995 Ukraine trip came to an end, I was asked, 'What are you going to do when we get back?' I had not thought that far forward, but without thought I responded, 'I'm going to get a job.' I'd been on unemployment benefit for two years by that time, but things were about to change again. People's expectations seemed to be for me to go straight back into the mission field and evangelizing, and I would have been happy to, but God had a few lessons in store for me before that was to happen again.

Chapter 9

Christianity in the Workplace

During a visit to a Christian bookshop I decided to buy one of those little fish emblems that many Christians wear. Mine had some Greek letters fixed in the middle of it. I could not work out whether or not I was wearing it the right way round, so I popped into a shop owned by one of my elders and asked him. He said, 'Colin, is this the extent of your problems?' We chuckled, but that was actually the truth of the matter.

However, on my return from Ukraine, that was about to change. I arrived back at my accommodation on the Friday night, knowing deep within my heart that I would be getting a job very soon. A few years earlier, I had chosen to allow my heavy-duty licence to expire. I had simply not renewed it. I had a terrible employment record and was blacklisted for numerous thefts from numerous delivery points and/or from my diesel tank. I had accepted that losing the HGV licence was a consequence of my former lifestyle.

I had been working part time for the Morris family, driving a van delivering engineering parts. The part-time job helped me to keep in touch with employment commitment without too much responsibility too fast. The Morris family belong to God and they are a very gracious bunch. They understood my need of slow growth, and allowed me two or three days' work a week. It also helped me to start interacting in the workplace as a new Christian – something else I needed to do gradually.

As I started to mature, I started to miss the truck driving, with feelings of frustration because I knew 'I could do it honestly now'. When I woke up on the Saturday morning after Ukraine, I had the idea to phone the driving licence people in Swansea, just to enquire how to go about getting my licence back. It made no sense to ring these people because it was Saturday. I rang, though, deciding that the worst-case scenario would be to leave a message on the system until Monday.

I was surprised when the phone was answered, and I was even more surprised when the guy who answered the phone went straight into his computer to find my details, and within minutes he told me, 'Sir, your licence is current and valid; there is no problem with it.' I just stared at the phone in my hand, because this was unbelievable.

Trucking

I left my flat that morning with an added spring in my step. I felt that doors of employment were about to open for me, and this time I could do it all honestly. I noticed a truck with a Stroud address passing through the village I was living in and decided to follow it. The thought of trucking was very exciting in a new kind of way. I had started to learn to manage my finances whilst on unemployment benefits, to the extent of saving in a Post Office account. The banks rejected my applications as soon as my name came up on their computers. I accepted all these knock-backs with peace, embracing them as something I would just have to live with. I had robbed from everyone around me, to the point of emptying my chequebook on electrical goods and clothes, knowing that there was nothing in my account. I had to find peace in my heart that my life might never reach anything like normal, and a willingness to face the banks about my former dishonesties. But first I had to be in a position where I could actually do something to repay, should they so desire. I was ready. I was prepared to work for nothing if it meant I could repay all I had defrauded.

I followed that truck back to its depot and was met by the boss of the company. Within two minutes of talking to him, he had employed me, starting on the Monday at 5.00 a.m. I could see that I was slowly getting back all that had been destroyed. On the Sunday night I was fired up with nervous anticipation and could not sleep. As the night turned into early morning, I started to grow in anxiety. 'I have to sleep,' was the thought that kept me awake. I was dreading having to read a map, find delivery points, interact with earthlings and handle a 16-ton truck. I was licensed to drive up to 30 tons, but because I had been off the road for so long, I went back in with the small stuff.

The rain had fallen very steadily all night. Believe me, I listened to it. It was pouring down. I was gradually growing in dread to the point of thinking, 'I'm not going. I simply cannot do it.' I curled up in a ball on my bed and, like a little child, I said, 'Lord, I don't want to go to work in this rain.' At that very moment, it stopped raining. It had poured for hours, and as soon I got childlike before God, the rain stopped. I just knew God was on my side. In the midst of all my anxiety, I had forgotten. But there he was, just waiting for me to ask in the right way.

I got the sense that the Lord himself had actually caused the rain to stop just for me. This was not something for me to testify about. I knew that even among Christians, this would be treated with amusement. This was God himself interacting with me personally. As I curled up in a small ball on my bed, he took my heart to the truth of Sovereignty. And yet, in contrast to seeing him in any position of power or dominion, I saw a tenderly swollen brow attacked by thorns, and muscles stretched beyond their limit. I saw a naked and twisted human form with its ribcage on show for the counting, and a slow rise and fall of a blood-soaked chest in its final attempts for an air intake. I saw Jesus in a whole new light. I saw that all things had been created by him and for him, and that in his way he was reconciling all things back to himself. I saw that he had even created the atmospheric dynamics that engineered the cloud formation that produced this rain, and it was at his bidding that the rain started and stopped.

I then saw another cloud formation, hundreds of years before Christ was born, in its infancy, yet fast maturing and moistening to produce millions, probably billions of raindrops, more than man's most advanced technology could ever count or even estimate. Look at it this way: a million seconds is eleven days, but a billion seconds is thirty-two years, and in amongst these myriads of raindrops, one specific droplet was appointed to land upon one specific seed. That seed absorbed that raindrop, and a new form of life started its cycle and purpose. A tiny stem, slowly thickening and producing leaves. Years of growth, with varying seasonal climates, and only God will ever know how many more raindrops were drunk by that seed. God produced the means and purpose for the growth of that seed.

Until, one day, believing the initiative to be his own, man cut down that tree. Then in accordance with God's foreknowledge and plan, they stripped and carved that tree. Both lumberjack and carpenter had received their skills for this purpose from this God. Then finally, and once again for God's ultimate purpose, an instrument of torture was created from that tree. The cross was made, for the crucifixion of his own dear Son on Calvary. All pre-ordained and carefully fulfilled in order for the likes of Colin Garnett to climb into a trash can full of water in a prison chapel with his sinful soul, and go free from the bondages of sin and its life-controlling consequences of addiction. Even, it could be argued, so that I could curl up into a small ball on my bed in the early hours of the morning, and selfishly worry about going to work in the rain, in order to gain more depth of insight and gratitude.

By 5:30 that same morning I stood with my new employer, telling him, 'This is the day that the Lord has made.' He looked at me like I had no right to be so happy so early on a Monday morning, but I also detected a hint of envy in his eye. There was no way he could have known how I had been conveyed from a gory story to a glory story, but I could see that he saw something he liked. I left the depot that day with hitch-hikers and the gospel in mind. I was heading from Stroud to South Wales on the M5.

I drew into the first service station five minutes outside of Stroud. I did not stop at the service station; I simply drove through and picked up a guy on the exit slip-road. As he climbed into the cab, his body odour preceded him, a bit like an aura. I thought for a moment that he would probably have his own swarm of flies in the summer! He was very untidy, and not the best-looking guy in town. His face was weather-beaten and cruelly scarred by years of street life. By the time I had dropped him off on the other side of the Severn Bridge in Wales, I had delivered what I knew to be a very powerful and cutting gospel message. The guy just sat staring at me and   listening with an amazed expression on his face. I felt that my tattoos had become the backdrop of his expectations, but as I unpacked the meditations of my heart, the words of my mouth sort of hypnotized him. He simply could not make sense of it, and he looked like a rabbit trapped in headlights; he had nowhere to run.

Before he got out of the truck I asked if I could pray with him. During the prayer, the guy started to sob. I was sitting in the driver's seat, with one hand stretched across to rest on his shoulder. He cried for a good twenty minutes, about his failures and about his hopelessness, about his drinking and about his failed marriages. He spoke of rejection and loneliness in such a way that I could only listen and quietly cry along with him. In the end I had to anticipate the next lull and jump in to interrupt him, because I had work to do.

He turned to God that morning and humbled himself under the truth of who he was in relation to God's holiness. As I drove away, I caught a glimpse of him in my wing mirror. He looked totally different to when I had picked him up just under an hour before, and I just knew his life was never going to be the same again. I could not help but think that even his posture had changed, as if now he had purpose and direction. He wanted a lift to Wales and I was able to get him to Wales. However, what he had not bargained for was going via Bethlehem, Gethsemane, Calvary, God's Wrath, the Sacrificial Blood, God's Satisfaction, Death's Disarmament, the Empty Tomb and Glory's Invitation.

The rain had started again outside the truck and I was crying on the inside, and for some weird reason I turned the wipers on too fast, as if that would clear my vision. I had to pull the truck over to the side of the road because I was howling with laughter and joy, excitement and praise, and wonder at how God would use a toe-rag like me to redeem souls. I felt a deep excitement about being involved in the rescue of souls from the very clutches of evil and hell itself. I'd seen an awakening to the truth in Prison 62 in Ukraine, and I saw the very same illumination in the eyes of my scruffy little hitchhiker just off the M5 in Wales.

The weeping subsided eventually and I was able to get on with my job. As I did so, though, a burden was sprouting within me. I knew that the hitch-hiker would be looked after, just as I had been in prison and the guys in Ukraine's Prison 62 would be. The question starting to grow in my heart was, 'Did the Holy Spirit convict him of sin; or did I just impress and convince him towards God?' The Lord showed me that man operates by means of impression and convincing, but the Holy Spirit's primary role in the heart of an unregenerate sinner is to depress and convict.

Before this thought from God was over, I was starting to weep again. I reached a point that day where I wanted to say to God something along the lines of, 'Lord, will you back off a bit, please – I have got to get this job done!' Inwardly I knew that the Lord totally understood. I was struggling to understand grace, to the point of not wanting any more. Many times my thoughts would be, 'Lord, just go easy on the grace.' I knew heaven smiled over me, and the scruffy little hitch-hiker would be the first of many.

I worked for six months for this particular company, and on a number of occasions my boss set me a schedule which would require me to drive over the legal limit of hours. I had to stay within the law, and that meant I sometimes would not get the job done. I knew this would render me unpopular, even to the point of never making any progress in terms of promotion. I would always be last choice for any of the attractive jobs like overnight runs to Scotland. So before I knew it, I had gone as far as I was going to go in this job. Being out on the road each day gave me the opportunity to see who was who in the transport field. It turned out that probably the biggest transport company in the west of England had its base less than two miles from where I was stationed. I knew I could not work for this current employer much longer, because by standing firm in not breaking the law, I was growing in unpopularity.

It was early one Saturday morning when the bubble burst. Once again I had been set a task that was obviously legally impossible. I tried to explain that I would not get everything done within my legal hours. The boss just 'ordered' me to 'get on with it'. I threw the keys to him and simply said, 'No, you get on with it.' I walked out of that depot at 7 a.m. that Saturday morning. I visited the largest transport company in the west of England at 9 a.m. and started working for that company at 6 a.m. the following Monday. I felt that the Lord had honoured my desires for holiness and had opened the door to this job.

But within one week of starting, and being in the enviable position of working for such a company, I was inwardly feeling uneasy. Nothing can compare with sharing the gospel of Jesus Christ with lost souls. I was now working for the type of haulage company that I used to dream about in my earlier miserable attempts at employment. I used to believe, 'If I could just get a start with a company like that, I would be all right.' But now, here I was, and all it offered was a worldly type of satisfaction.

I sat in a transport café one morning, with a nice new truck outside and a pocket full of money. All around me I could see men of the world. All they spoke about was speed-traps, roadworks, breakdowns and fog-banks.

They spoke in a special kind of dialogue, and grew fat on greasy breakfasts. Hell was yawning beneath them, and ignorance was their best and only defence.

Every time I rang my new boss back at the office, it seemed that he was not happy until he had made some sort of disgusting sexual innuendo, and then roared with laughter at his own 'joke'. I found myself dreading the phone calls because I would always find myself with dirty images in my mind and feeling abused. I resolved to try and give this job two years, but God had another plan.

Back to the Ukraine

I had heard nothing from nor made any contact with Vic Jackopson for the remainder of 1995. I just tried to concentrate on work. I then heard via a newsletter that another Ukraine trip was being planned for the summer of 1996. Once again I joined the missionary team for another summer camp. I had developed a special bond with Trish and her husband Roy, and once again, back in Prison 62, I sat next to Trish as Vic took to the pulpit. He did it again. Vic opened God's Word, and God opened the hearts of everyone in the chapel.

Once again, I turned to Trish and said, 'He is sitting in my seat.'

Trish took on a serious tone and said quite sternly, 'Well then, you have to tell him.' I knew she was right.

Once again we saw many men get saved and Vic baptized many of the previous year's converts. It was all very beautiful, but it all felt kind of surreal to me, because I knew I had to approach this apostle-type preacher and tell him, 'I think you're sitting in my seat.' I was preoccupied for the rest of the day. That night I actually tried to avoid Vic. However, I saw that he was retiring for the night and I knew I had to get a move on.

I gently tapped on his door, inwardly hoping he would-n't hear, but just as gently he said, 'Come in.' We sat oppo-site each other in a room not too dissimilar to an average prison cell in the UK. There were two single beds. He sat on one and I sat on the other and we stared at each other. I could not help noticing that his feet did not reach the floor, but I saw a giant of a man before me. I went for it:

'Vic, at worst I am about to make a fool of myself. Please hear me out, and let me voice my heart to you.' I think I drank from the peace I saw in Vic's beautiful eyes, and with that I said, 'I think you might be keeping a seat warm for me.'

Vic sat back with a slow intake of breath and thought for a moment. He then said the strangest thing: 'Colin, education is of the utmost importance. You will always have a message for the drunk, the prisoner and the thug. But the gospel of Jesus Christ is aimed at the rich and the poor. The uneducated and the educated alike. Unless you sharpen up, you will lose many who need saving.'

I very nearly understood him. Then after a long apos-tolic stare and silence, he said, 'Have you ever consid-ered going to Bible College?'

I had to concede that I did not even know there was such a thing as Bible College. Another pause, but this time there was an eruption of excitement building in me. As Vic very politely opened the door for me to leave, he simply said, 'Try Moorlands.'

Before I knew it, I was outside his room and Trish was glowing with excitement in the corridor. 'What did he say?'

All I could say was, 'I'm going to Moorlands Bible College.'

There was a beautifully musical type of 'Amen!' from Trish, and we both started to grow in excitement about my going to college. I had no money whatsoever, and no academic muscle to flex to anyone, but I knew I was going to Moorlands Bible College, and that was that. I did not know where it was or what they taught, but I knew I was going.

The next morning I felt like it was a ridiculous dream, and actually doubted God's involvement in it all. How was I going to find funding for Bible College when I couldn't even get a bank account? Trish once again put me straight. 'Colin, that is God's business. Stop worrying, you will be going to Bible College.'

I considered asking my church back in Stroud, but I knew it was a small fellowship and struggling with its own overheads. I was working and earning quite well, but the truth had to be acknowledged: my days of working for worldly people with worldly ways were over. I felt that the Lord had met the dreams of my heart in terms of wanting to work for a well-established haulage company, in order for me to know without doubt that the world had nothing to offer me. Souls were perishing in every street of every town I visited, and there was I, trucking nationwide on an ego trip, keeping the very Word of Life secret! It did not sound or feel right at all. When I returned to work, I resigned my position before I had contacted Moorlands.

On my return from Ukraine, I found a court order in my mail. I was being summonsed to court for failing to pay seven months' worth of Poll Tax. I went into shock. I did not even realize that I should have been paying Poll Tax. My bills had been sent to my previous two addresses after I had left. I had a bill for £350. That same week I appeared in the Magistrates' Court in Stroud. I was asked to take the Bible in my right hand and read from the card. I looked to the bench and quietly refused to do so. Once again my tattoos had created the mood, and the magistrate rolled her eyes and instructed me to explain myself.

I said: 'Ma'am, I actually belong to the Lord. Within this, his Word, Jesus himself made it plain that he did not want his followers to swear by heaven because it is God's throne, but to simply let our yes be yes and our no be no. Ma'am, he has my life in his hand, I can assure you; I will not be giving false witness.'

I was excused the oath, and made a declaration instead. Regarding the £350 outstanding Poll Tax bill, I was asked why I had such an amount unpaid and what my intentions were. I said, 'Ma'am, I can give you no excuses. That bill has grown through genuine ignorance and irresponsibility. I am prepared to repay this amount at your guiding. However, I feel it would be more beneficial if this bill was written off.'

There was a growing uneasiness in the courtroom. 'Why?' I was asked.

'Ma'am, I am in the process of bettering myself. I am walking with God and have been for the past four years. I am four years clean after over seventeen years of chronic heroin addiction. I am trying for Bible College this year. I could make you a commitment to pay this bill and lay aside college. Or I could make you a commitment to repay it from student status. I feel it would be a travesty if I were to lay college aside for a relatively small amount, and I also feel it would be naïve to think I could honour dual commitments, when college is going to demand my all.'

The courtroom was the quietest I had ever heard a courtroom to be. The magistrate asked me, 'What would you suggest?'

'Please write off the debt, Ma'am.'

Without further question or thought, as if she had already made up her mind, the magistrate placed my file back in its folder and said, 'Outstanding debt in this case to be withdrawn. Case dismissed. Mr Garnett, I have a funny feeling you are going to do well. Enjoy college.'

I left the courtroom and walked beside a local canal. I was in a state of deep internal communion with and worship of God. I had not yet contacted college. I was so wrapped up in the very fact that God was always one step ahead of me; I was half expecting them to contact me. I rang them and made an appointment for an interview. I was very excited about getting back into a classroom environment, but not before I had interviewed them.

College interview

I went to Moorlands College in August of 1997 for an interview, and it was much more than I had anticipated. Surrounded by beautiful countryside, in its own tranquil setting and within ten minutes of England's south coast, I could not have asked for more. I sat with two of the lecturers and we just chatted at a very superficial level to begin with. I was asked what academic qualifications I had, because there were certain criteria that one had to meet in order to qualify for a Bachelor of Arts Degree course. I was mind-blown by it all. I wasn't interested in getting a BA Degree; I just wanted to study God's Word and broaden my horizons of influence with the gospel. The thought of doing a Bachelor of Arts Degree was simply too much for me to contemplate.

I simply said, 'I have no academic background to talk about whatsoever.' I gave a ten-minute testimony, and then said, 'All I know is, I'm coming to this college.' I was asked who had recommended Moorlands to me, and when I said Vic Jackopson, the meeting was adjourned for lunch.

When we reconvened, one of the lecturers had a very reassuring smile for me. We sat and he explained: 'Colin, in this day and age one does not simply walk into a college and say, "I am coming to this college." One has to have a certain academic standard to begin with. Such is the demand for Bachelor of Arts Degree courses, one is required to have a minimum of two A-levels. We cannot, therefore, offer you our three-year degree course. How would you feel about doing a two-year diploma in theology?'

I allowed my heart to speak. 'Sir, two years is not going to be long enough. It will take me two years to learn how to learn. What else can you suggest?'

I was told to go away and pray about it and ring them the next day. When I rang, I was told: 'Well, for some time now this college has been considering running a four-year degree course, starting with a foundation year, which would qualify one for a three-year degree. It has to be said that your case has caused us to re-open this idea. In fact, we feel you are the catalyst for the introduction of this course, and we would love to offer you a place starting in September.'

I did not need to pray or think any further; I simply accepted. As soon as I put the phone down from that call, and without realizing how important it was to me, I rang my family and told them. The deep desire to impress them was still there. The only response I got from my dad was a swear-word. He rang me back a few hours after I had told him, when it had sunk in, and he said, 'Son, that is the best news I have had since your mum died.'

I cried. It was lovely. I said, 'Promise me you won't die before I graduate.' He promised. My plea to God was, 'Please let him enjoy this!' Every member of my family was overwhelmed with joy and admiration. All the broken promises and failings of the past suddenly meant nothing.

I was being offered a second attempt at school. I sat before God that night and simply bowed before him for his goodness, grace, mercy, faithfulness, kindness and provision. I was sat silent before this awesome Father God, and the eyes of my heart exploded with the light of his character.

Chapter 10

Moorlands College

Sitting on my desk as I write, I have the first book I purchased at the outset of four years of theological studies, *The Ladybird Book of Spelling and Grammar For Children*. On the wall directly behind me as I write hangs a certificate which reads:

This is to certify that
Colin Garnett
Has been awarded the degree of
Bachelor of Arts
Having followed an approved honours
programme in
Applied Theology

Hope Now Ministries met me, accepted me, trusted in me, loved me and wanted the best for me. They financially covered me for four years of theological training, supporting me in my need for books and a car. This was, and still is, active Christianity and faithful stewarding of God's funds.

I was warned prior to Bible College that theological study could destroy a man's faith. I had to bounce back with, 'Group therapy in jail should have broken me, but it didn't.' I had no worries about my faith; I was just intimidated about joining a group of 'straights' for four years. How would I react to them?

At the start of college, we were told that we had to reach a pass mark of 40 per cent per assignment. For my first few assignments I was struggling to reach this standard, but I was getting there, and I thought it was only going to improve. I set myself a goal: if, by the end of college, I could be reaching 50 per cent or more, I would have made ample progress.

Being in the classroom environment was very refreshing for me. God's grace was very evident to me and I felt like I was drinking in every word the lecturers said. I was actually studying God's Word, all day, with the help of learned people. I soon started to realize how little I knew.

Over a four-year period I heard some wonderful sermons from some of God's most heavily anointed men. I saw men weeping whilst praying over lunch. I took part in wonderful worship. I felt people loving me even when I was at my most unlovely, and I felt myself sinking deeper in love with Jesus the Nazarene. My theological standpoint gained stability and growth, and my understanding of relationships took on a whole new depth.

Altrincham Priory

Part of our Level 2 curriculum was to find a five-week, hands-on practical placement. The norm was to find a church placement for experience of working in the church context. I knew in an instant – with the same assurance that I had felt when I knew that I was going to Moorlands and that Jesus was calling me – that I was going to work in one of the treatment clinics where I had been sent by the court in 1991. It just went without saying; working in a church never even entered the theatre of thought for me.

I rang a clinic in Manchester – Altrincham Priory – and asked if they could accommodate me for five weeks while I undertook a fact-gathering mission. I acknowledged their programme and the wonderful effect it had had on me.

I also said, 'I believe that you boast a 70 per cent success rate over addictions, but that the fees are extraordinarily high. I therefore believe that in charging so much for treatment, you are actually marginalizing 70 per cent of the people you profess to want to reach in addiction and alcoholism. My long-term goal is to sit in and watch what you do and to learn as much as I can from you, so that I can go and do likewise for the marginalized free of charge.'

I was warmly invited to join their team for five weeks, on condition that I respected their 'freedom of religion' ethos, and that I did not preach Christ over any other belief system. For some weird reason, I knew God wanted me in there and I simply agreed.

I went up to Manchester and simultaneously invested in my family reconciliation. My family had been ravaged by my addiction for a very long time. Healing was a long process, and going to Manchester was all part of it. I stayed with my sister Linda and her husband Ged.

Years earlier, at the height of my addiction, I stole some cash from Linda's bedroom. Ged knew it was me, but I managed once again to convince Linda that I was innocent. Some weeks later, when the guilt weighed too heavily upon me, I went back and confessed. This was very damaging. Linda and Ged had argued over my guilt, and Linda had sided with me, saying, 'I know when my baby brother is lying.'

My confession was not born in sorrow. I was selfishly wanting them to forgive me so that I could be free from the guilt. Their marriage very nearly hit the rocks because of this and some similar incidents. But now I was clean from drugs and was studying at Bible College, and the wounds were healing. They opened their home to me.

At the clinic I sat in the small-group environment and watched as the counsellors systematically dismantled the denial systems from around the hearts and minds of addicts and alcoholics, by the gentle application of simple truth. I sat silently for five weeks. I spoke to no one about Jesus Christ. I returned to a feeling I had felt when I was in treatment. I looked at the counsellors and knew in my heart that I could do what they did, with equal or perhaps more effectiveness.

I returned to college at the end of my five weeks to find that my Placement Supervisor's report said: 'Colin does not have to preach his belief; he lives it.' This came from a female version of P.J. McCullough. Her name was Wynne Parry, a very spiritual lady who stood for no nonsense either from her patients or their families. She, like PJ, was an expert in her field.

I was daily locked into one line of thought: 'This style of treatment would be ideal for making disciples.' It went directly to deeply rooted attitudes, pointing out pride and shame, fear and guilt, lust and envy, anger and fear.

During my final year of Bible College, Hope Now offered me the position of Head of Prison Ministry. I felt it was right to accept this position, even entertaining the possibility of starting prisoner treatment-style disciple-ship courses, applying everything I had gathered in my remoulding experiences in therapy. Vic asked if I would like to go to Cape Town to visit Pollsmoor Prison. Hope Now was supporting two ministers out there and it was a steadily growing ministry.

Suddenly, with the offer, I became the boss of people I had never met, so it seemed right to visit. My studies in the final year grew in intensity, but I was feeling inwardly confident that I was going to go the distance. My grades were higher than the standard which I had set myself, and it started to feel like a downhill ride.

South Africa

In April 2000, I went to Cape Town. The two ministers had prepared an itinerary for me that kept me on the go pretty much all the time. I gave my testimony in several different sections of the prison, and each time I finished, a very fiery altar call was made. Every time the altar call went out, 98 per cent of those listening put their hands up to 'receive Christ'. I felt inwardly sceptical. Was it this easy? Is Satan so easily beaten? Can the one who is described by God as being 'full of wisdom' be robbed of souls just like that?

I also gave testimony at seventeen churches in sixteen days. We went flat out and I nearly burned out. I found myself feeling deeply frustrated at giving testimony to the captive audiences of prison, whose motives are influenced by a desire to look good in the eyes of parole boards, especially to be seen as becoming a Christian. But I felt equally frustrated about giving testimony to Christians. I started to feel like I was in the entertainment business. I grew inwardly confused.

Towards the end of the South Africa visit, I told my hosts that I was taking a break. I had just over a week left and I had had no time out. It had been said in the prison ministry office that week, 'Oh, we must find Colin a South African wife before he leaves!'

I reacted by laughing it off and saying, 'Forget it, guys! I don't want a South African wife, thanks very much.'

I often entertained the idea of marriage, but felt quite at ease with singleness if that was God's desire for me. I was certainly not in the shop-window. I had actually shaved my head and looked very thuggish, so I was adamant that it was not going to happen on this trip.

Unknown to me, I was supposed to speak for fifteen minutes at Meadowridge Baptist Church in the evening on Sunday 9 April 2000. This was the night the Lord gave me a wife!

I had given full testimonies at all the other churches. I really went for it for fifty minutes. The minister, Revd John Broome, at the end simply stood up and said, 'Amen and good night!' I left the stage exhausted.

I had become aware of a deep hypocrisy in me at previous venues. After each testimony, it was expected that as the speaker, I would shake hands with, sometimes, up to 400 people. I was all right for the first ten or fifteen people, but then in my heart I was thinking one thing but saying another. I was smiling, but only on the outside. I was being false, and feeling forced into a position of prestige and power. It just happens. One inwardly starts to feel like something one isn't. I hated it. I found myself saying 'thank you' to the congregation members, but in my heart I was wishing myself to be somewhere else.

Deanna

So after the Meadowridge service that night, I decided to avoid the crowd. I slid out of the side door and noticed a huge cross on the outside wall. I inwardly smiled and sat at the foot of the cross. I had gone from the pulpit to an inner attitude of sin. I needed the cross. I had sat there for five minutes and was contemplating going back in when I heard the door open. A lady walked out holding a Bible under her arm. We almost bumped into each other at the foot of that cross. We exchanged polite nods and nervous smiles, me not having a clue what to say.

The lady then said, 'Thank you for your testimony; I feel like I have turned a corner tonight. I have been feeling far from God, but your talk has brought the reality of his love home to me.'

I thought something along the lines of 'Wow, man!'

Not at her testimony; it was her eyes. I almost fell into them. We chatted for a moment and it came out that she was involved in a family business in vehicle and motor-home hire. When I heard this, I pictured a mobile home, like a big caravan. I told her that the prison ministry was looking for a classroom for the young prisoners, and I gave her my phone number in case she thought she might be able to help us.

As she walked away, I confess, I quickly checked the chassis out, before remembering the hovering cross. I apologized to the Lord, saying, 'Lord, I'm fine if you want me single, but if in your mercy you say I can have a wife, can I have one just like that?'

I had also taken her number. I was also smitten by her name: Deanna. I said it a few times throughout the next few days.

Then on Thursday 13 April, she rang. I can't remember talking about a classroom for the young prisoners. In all honesty, I couldn't have cared less about the prisoners at that moment. *She rang me, she rang me, she rang me!*

Deanna very politely suggested that if I had any spare time during the next few days and wanted to get away from the madding crowds and see more of Cape Town, we could possibly go out for a meal.

I said, 'How about tomorrow?'

Deanna said, 'What about Saturday?'

I said, 'OK, Saturday, then.'

I was flying back to England on the Tuesday, so some

time out was due, and what better way to see Cape Town than with a very attractive local girl?

Deanna and I went to Cape Town's Waterfront for a meal. It was simply romantic and very romantically simple. We sat and chatted about the Waterfront, the various cultures, the shape of the wine-glass, the meal, and the pudding. We sat and chatted about 'things'. The simple things in life, and as we did so, I felt my heart getting warmer and warmer towards her. I was not asked one question about my past or me. Deanna was not interested in who I used to be or who I was being portrayed as by the church – as a wonderful living proof of God's grace. Deanna was simply interested in me, Colin, and it totally blew me away. I got a break from me for the evening and I saw exactly what I was starved of – acceptance for who I was as an individual. Deanna and I left the restaurant and walked into the Waterfront.

Cape Town's Waterfront is one of the city's high points. Everyone who visits Cape Town visits the Waterfront. Deanna and I sat on a bench, facing the ugliest building for miles. It has to be said that we only had eyes for each other. It was during this part of the evening that I asked her about her family. With a little chuckle, Deanna told me that her dad was originally from Bristol. He was a policeman! It flashed through my mind that I had been set up and there was a camera hidden somewhere. We both just laughed. A copper's kid. Trust me! My lengthy testimony in Meadowridge Baptist Church included all the violence, all the jails, all the drugs, all the overdoses, delivered with a shaven head – and I go out and meet a copper's kid, at the foot of the cross! I used to terrorize coppers' kids. This is what it means when it is said that the ground at the foot of the cross of Christ is level. Names, histories, reputations and academic achievement, good or bad, mean nothing in the shadow of the cross of Jesus Christ.

Deanna went on to tell me that she studied and graduated in Law, and the poetic irony of the situation grew in colour and detail. Deanna could in no way whatsoever identify with the things she had heard going on in my life, but in a wonderful way, she identified with me. She could not relate to the sins, but could relate with the sinner. That night Deanna was reminded loud and clear that God loved her and was interested in her.

I arranged with my hosts that Deanna would be taking me to the airport for my flight home on the Tuesday. We prayed together in the departure lounge of Cape Town International Airport for God's will to be made plain to us. It was a very beautiful time, until I had to leave. I went through the final check-in gate and turned to say goodbye. As we said goodbye, Deanna made the move and walked away. I knew, right there and then, that this was not goodbye. I did not sleep a wink on that flight home and Deanna was at the forefront of my thoughts for every moment of the journey. I forced her out from time to time to pray, but I was bitten.

I rang Deanna two days later from England. I explained to her that I could not get involved in a relationship with her for entertainment's sake and it therefore had to be with a view to getting married, if at all. I then said, 'So the ball is now in your court.' It had to be the world's most feeble marriage proposal.

Deanna was having none of it, though, and she immediately put the onus back on me. 'What do you mean?'

I closed my eyes and said, 'Will you marry me?'

With my eyes still closed, I waited for her answer – and she said she would!

One week later, Deanna arrived at Heathrow Airport. We agreed to go through the seasons together before tying that knot. Dee found a job in London and we got together each weekend, and we slowly go to know each other. It was a beautiful time.

My family in Manchester grew more and more secure in their love and respect for me. I had not yet met Deanna's family. All of a sudden their daughter/sister had jetted off to England to be with this guy who proposed after one week. This normally stoic and quite reserved lady, who had never rushed into anything in her whole life, had met and agreed to marry an ex-con.

A short time after Deanna arrived, I suggested phoning her dad to ask for his blessing on our marriage. We went out for lunch one Sunday afternoon, and from the reception area of the hotel restaurant, I rang him and asked, 'Sir, I would like to ask you for your daughter's hand in marriage.'

Derek Iles, formerly second-in-command of the British South Africa Police (BSAP) in Zimbabwe, considered dragging me over the coals for ten or fifteen minutes of torment, but conceded that both he and his wife, Ethnie, felt at peace about the whole scenario, and he expressed great pleasure in handing Deanna, their only daughter, over to me for engagement to be married. We set the date for the following Easter season, 14 April 2001, at Meadowridge Baptist Church, Cape Town.

For my final year of studies, I once again had to find a five-week hands-on practical placement for myself, starting in February 2001. It seemed to go without saying, because of my new Hope Now appointment as Head of Prison Ministry, that Cape Town would meet several needs, the first one being that of getting to meet my new fiancée's family. As soon as college broke up for Christmas, I flew out to Cape Town once again and we all started getting to know each other and planning for the wedding. The Iles family took me in as one of their own right from the start. They converted what used to be a garage into a little flat for me, and I lived in it for the duration of my block placement. I was instantly amazed at how easy these guys were to get along with. We all went away for the Christmas period and I caught glimpses of beautiful South Africa, and started getting to know 'the folks'.

My college placement was due to start on 5 January, and in all honesty, I could not find peace in my heart about working in the prison. It all sounded logical, considering my prison background, but it would not settle in me that this was going to be God's plan for me. I kept getting images of everyone in the room lifting their hands 'to receive Jesus', and with that image came a deep burden as to the authenticity of these 'conversions' and what would happen to them next. I believe every conversion to Christ has to produce fruit – instant fruit. A change in attitude toward God, self and others. I felt these conversions were in the extreme minority. And so I prayed about what to do.

Beth Rapha

On Christmas day, Deanna and I, along with her mum and dad, went to St James' Church in Kenilworth, Cape Town. It was a lovely service with a wonderful gospel message. During the service, an announcement was given about a donation they had received for Beth Rapha, 'our house in Observatory for men and women who have been ravaged by alcoholism and drug addiction'. Once again, in that part of me that just knows, I knew: *I am going to do my block placement at this Beth*

Rapha place.

After the service, I asked the minister of St James' about Beth Rapha, and he pointed me toward another guy, saying, 'Talk to him.' I approached the guy and introduced myself, asking if he was running Beth Rapha.

He laughed and said, 'Brother, I'm not running it; I'm just limping forward from day to day, waiting for God to send help.'

I gave him a two-minute testimony and in that time, I saw the colour fall out of his face. I thought he had seen something behind me, such was the change in his expression.

When I finished talking, he very quietly said: 'We have been waiting for you. When can you start?'

That afternoon, Deanna and I took a ride into Observatory, and we found number 4 Grant Street. It was sitting in the middle of an area blighted by drug addiction, alcoholism and prostitution. I parked the car outside the house and inwardly started to freeze. The front door of the house was open and I could see right into the lounge area. The floor had no carpet, the walls had no paint, and the prospect of walking into this dark, cave-like place caused me to tremble. I could see two men on the inside, both glazed from drugs and both itching with what must surely be fleabites.

In my heart of hearts, I said: 'Lord, please do not send me in there!' In all the glamour of travel and speaking at so many venues, and climbing onto a self-created pedestal, I had forgotten something: a while ago I had prayed, 'Lord, I want to take this testimony right into the enemy's backyard!' Then right at that moment, I felt like the Holy Spirit was saying something along the lines of: 'Colin, I felt just like you do now, just before I walked into your heart and set you free.'

I walked into that darkness without further thought and sat down. I was acutely aware of fleas and skin diseases, of blood on the carpets and of eyes full of manipulation and sadness. For every face, I saw an inner desperation that I knew so well. I heard their hard-luck stories, and their declarations of defeat in the area of addiction, but it was the extreme sense of hopelessness that I saw that spoke to me the most. These guys had nothing. They had no one to turn to for support of any kind any more, because they had ripped off just about everyone they knew, one time too many. This was the end of the line.

In the other treatment centres I had visited, I had seen the wealthiest failures anyone could wish to meet. They were all in the exact same state of inner desperation and hopelessness as the men before me, yet they had good healthcare and families with limitless funds. The guys at Beth Rapha were from shop doorways and were involved in chronic alcoholism, prostitution, physical and sexual abuse, gangs, murder and rape.

And there sat I, clean and as free as a bird, having Christ within, the hope of glory. I was also sitting on all the information any one of these wretches would need to get clean and sober. If I applied a tiny fraction of what I had experienced and learned from my time spent in treatment, going by the clinics' professed 70 per cent success rate, I should expect to see at least four of these guys get clean. I had sat in group therapy sessions with PJ back at Pierpoint House, and then again in my college placement at Altrincham Priory, and I had known inwardly that I could do what they did.

So now it was put-up-or-shut-up time for me. I had told the staff at Altrincham Priory, 'My long-term goal is to sit in and watch what you do and to learn as much as I can from you, so that I can go and do likewise for the marginalized, free of charge.' Now here I was, and

God had honoured his side of the vision he had given me.

I gave the people in that house that day a five-minute testimony of who I was, what had happened to me and what my life was now like. There was a very deep silence in that room as I declared that Jesus could rescue them from the darkest of personal dungeons, and these guys knew it was more than a sermon. It was a living and active testimony to the grace and power of the True and Living God, and the power of the cross of Christ, and the cleansing power of his blood, and the liberating power of God's Holy Spirit, bringing to life true forgiveness in Christ – all the stuff they had been exposed to at some point over the years in church services, but now, here was a life that declared that Jesus was personal and alive.

The presence of God in that place was something quite unusual. The guys sat in silence and listened intently to my testimony. After five minutes or so I said, 'Now, if you want me to come and help you I will, but that has to be your desire and request.'

In an instant I received a chorus of 'Please help us!'

I said I would have to pray about it before giving a final yes or no.

Deanna and I then went away for a week with her parents for a holiday. I did not think about Beth Rapha once during that week. God had sealed his decision in my heart, therefore it needed no further prayer. I just had to let college know that there had been a logistical change of plan. Before we broke up from college for that Christmas break, we were told that under no circumstances were we to change our block placement. I rang college from Cape Town and gave my supervising tutors, Peter Kingston and Colin Bennett, a brief testimony about Beth Rapha. I was given permission to make the change.

Not long after our return, Deanna and I attended the same church and I was asked to give a brief testimony in the evening service by the Bishop of South Africa. The Bishop got more than he bargained for with my testimony, and he invited Deanna and me out for coffee straight after the service.

Over coffee, Bishop Retief brought up Beth Rapha. It was proving a bit of a problem for this middle-class church to cope with. When I informed him that I had visited the house, he was delighted. He asked, 'What do you think we should do with it?'

I said, 'Drop it like a hot spud. Get rid of it. Give it back to the world and take the Name of Jesus off the door. It is a spiritual cesspit, a terrible witness and unworthy of such a great Name.'

I got the impression that what he had already experienced had opened up the same channel of thought. He asked if there were any alternatives.

I simply said, 'Why not let me run it for five weeks?' I went on, 'If nothing changes, then get rid of it; but let me have it for five weeks and see what happens.'

We shook hands, and I knew that it was time for action. I rang Beth Rapha that night and told Malcolm, the guy in charge of the place, that I would be there at 8.00 a.m. sharp, Monday, 3 January, offering one guarantee: *change*. Malcolm gave me a very deep chuckle.

I walked in and saw about fourteen expectant faces on that first morning at Beth Rapha. I did not have a plan and I did not have a clue in what direction it was going. I just knew that Christ lived in me, and that he had rescued me from this very same deep, dark valley. I was back in the valley of death from which he had redeemed me. I'd told him I wanted to go back in, and here I was, fleas and all.

So now what? I had five weeks to make an impact. However, God made a start that same day. I decided to start off as I meant to carry on, and therefore I told one of the guys in the kitchen to put the kettle on for a cup of tea. Everyone seemed to relax a bit and two guys set about making fifteen cups of tea. As I watched, I saw an opening. One guy asked for five sugars! Five sugars? Then another asked for three and another asked for four. I had forgotten that when one first comes off the drug or hasn't had any for a few hours, two things wake up: a sweet tooth and the sex drive.

I sat the guys down and we started to chat. I steered them to a place of agreement that they were in a good place, where they had a bed, food, tea, hot water, cold water, bread and sugar. We started what I now know to be 'thank you therapy'. We started counting our blessings. We were all feeling very grateful when I said how fortunate we were to be off the street where people were dying of murder, hunger and suicide. The old and cracked faces on these young men started to see things in a different way.

Two sugars or die

Then just as the guys were starting to open their hearts and minds to the truth of the poverty and decay around them, I said, 'From now on, there is a limit of two sugars every time you have a drink of tea in this house.'

I left the silence to linger for a good minute. The guys seemed to sense that things were about to change.

'From this point, if you want to get free from the life-controlling plague and the soul-destroying influence of alcoholism and heroin addiction; if you want to receive God's richest blessings upon your life, and to see your families restored and your children's eyes once again smiling at you; and if you truly want to see a Christmas without having to go to oblivion to enjoy it, then it is this simple: *two sugars in your tea.*'

With that I left for the day. I went back to Deanna's place, and took a swim in the pool. I lay sunbathing all on my own and underwent several manic outbursts of roaring laughter, as I slowly started to see what God was doing at Beth Rapha. Later that day, Malcolm rang me simply to say, 'I trust you, brother, and I think I know what you are doing.' We laughed like crazy. I was 20 kilometres away, diving in and out of my future in-laws' swimming pool, soaking up the sun, with not one solitary care in the world, and I had a whole house full of drug addicts, gangsters and alcoholics, staring at each other, not knowing what the hell was going on.

I got there at 8:00 a.m. on the dot the next day and we started by having a group therapy session. We prayed for a few minutes and then a silence fell. After a few minutes, I started to stir up the urgency for honesty in this ministry:

'Whatever the truth is about your thoughts, your feelings or your behaviour, the one conquering factor can and will only ever be the truth. Addiction has an engine-room and it is dishonesty. As long as dishonesty exists, there will always be the probability of falling back into full-blown addiction, hospitals, mental institutions, prisons and eventually death. Dishonesty has raped you and your families, and they live today, fearing your return and your dishonesty.'

I did not see one eye blink. I drove it home for ten or fifteen minutes and there was not a sound from anyone else in that room. Eventually I sat back and allowed a new depth of silence to settle upon us. Then very quietly I said:

'Who had more than two sugars in their tea in the early hours of this morning?'

Now it made sense. Faces went really pale.

One guy put his hand up and I quickly responded with: 'I am going to give you two warnings: (1) More than two sugars once more, and I will put you back on the street. (2) You will be using drugs before the end of the month.'

I got a very angry reaction from most of the residents, telling me it was a stupid rule and it meant nothing if a person had more than two sugars in their tea. I then explained that God had a deep desire to transform their lives into something brand new and to give them sweet fellowship with his Son Jesus and to set them free, but he was unable to. He was actually disqualified from helping them, because he could see that when no one else was looking, they were dishonest. I then promised on God's behalf that as soon as they could be honest when no one was looking, for no other reason than a hunger and thirst to be righteous, God would fulfil his purposes in their lives and they would go free.

I had spoken to Deanna the night before about one particular guy. His name was Brian. I saw burning hatred in Brian's eyes. He had long-term wounds and was a professional manipulator. He scared me. I had told Dee that I felt good about the task ahead, but felt totally hopeless around this Brian guy. I told her that I could not see any hope for this guy.

That week, as we sat in silence after a long chat about grace and the promise of freedom, Brian very quietly started to weep. His face became contorted with immense grief and pain, and suddenly the tears burst out of him. He became a sobbing wreck. The Holy Spirit simply unplugged his pent-up pain and out it all came.

I had to stop some guys from trying to comfort him because he needed to cry more than anything else in life.

He sobbed and sobbed. As he wept, one word came to mind: *leader*.

I believed that the Holy Ghost was starting on Brian. I quietly said, 'Let him cry. It is God's will that we each weep over our broken lives.'

At that, another guy started crying. Beth Rapha became a home of weeping for the whole of that morning. In that dirty run-down building, where the windows and the walls had turned a dirty smelly yellow colour from the years of nicotine and drug smoke, and where the carpet was now black and stuck to the floor, where cockroaches came out at night to devour anything they could and the rats were of a frightening size, God's Holy Spirit met with men. Later that day Brian sheepishly walked into my office and gave me his drug paraphernalia – syringes, spoons, the lot. He simply said, 'I have to get serious with this Jesus,' and walked out.

I simply sat and stared at the wall. God was moving where I had given up.

Fumigation

Each day when I returned to Dee's place, I stripped to my swimming costume whilst Dee fumigated me with a spray. I had seen scabies and fleas on practically all my friends at Beth Rapha, and I suddenly became aware of every itch and bite. Beth Rapha was a very dark place, but a morally moved leadership who visited twice a week with admirable ideals and plans could not run it by standing on the outside saying, 'This way, this way.' Someone was going to have to get in amongst the men and point to the only way out: the Innocent Nazarene who hanged on a tree, soaking up unto himself the punishment of the sins of every man within that Beth Rapha establishment.

Deanna and I attended the same church where we had heard about Beth Rapha, and we started to enjoy sitting under some very challenging teaching from God's Word. It was a middle-to-upper-class, predominantly white church, and more than once I looked around it and felt myself very blessed to be playing a tiny part in the ministry of such a prestigious church.

My five weeks' placement passed by very quickly, and before I knew it I was back at the airport, heading home. I had started to graft into Deanna's family, and I had witnessed God start a work at Beth Rapha. As I settled back into my seat on the flight home, several questions and concerns started to formulate. None more strongly than: 'If we are not careful and discerning, we could kill that ministry.' I had no idea whether or not I would play any further role at Beth Rapha, but I did know that the church alone was, unfortunately, underqualified to make it work. When I left, I knew that God had done enough already for it to grow, if it was allowed to. I knew it was going to take something like three years for this ministry to stabilize. Brian was in a position of trainee leader, now working alongside Malcolm, who himself had undergone some serious changes in heart and attitude.

Brian started to grow quickly – a little too quickly. Several times he would come into my office and absorb every word that came out of my mouth. I tried to warn him about focusing on me. He would say things like, 'Colin, I want what you have. I just want to be like you.' I tried and tried to point him away from me and to the Lord Jesus Christ. He needed to know Jesus personally as opposed to settling for a second-hand Christianity, feeding off the relationship I was having with the Lord.

Brian could not fully accept that Jesus Christ would want an intimate relationship with him. That was too much for him to believe.

Back to college

I returned to college on 7 February 2001. As the dust settled and 'student normality' returned, I woke to a new knowledge about my future. I could not accept the position of head of Hope Now International Prison Ministry. I grew in zeal for what I now saw as a need for 'contextualized discipleship'. In sending his disciples into 'all nations' to make disciples (Matt. 28:19–20), Jesus knew that cultural bridges would have to be built and then crossed. These bridges would have to enter not only various cultures, but also various contexts and mind-sets within those cultures. I had been formed and fashioned over a period of more than thirty-five years – first, the struggle and shame of an emotionally suppressed child in the lower-working-classes; then my reaction to that background, which led me through the hell and loneliness of addiction. Running a prison ministry, in my view, was not therefore the arena into which God wanted to place me.

I was haunted by the question of what happens before and, even more importantly, after prison. That dilemma, in my view, simply had to be addressed. I had been blessed with survival from that which had killed over twenty of my personal friends. Every time I revisited Stockport, another friend had died from addiction-related consequences. My whole being yearned to make a difference with Christ in addiction's pit of despair.

It was going to be a big decision to turn down the Hope Now job, because of the security it offered me and because of my heartfelt belief in Hope Now's ministry, but I had to be truthful and make way for a season away from them. I could only pray about it a while and sit and listen to what God was saying.

I got on with my final term of studies with a sense of excitement growing in me about the Beth Rapha experience. I felt a very strong pull toward residential-type discipleship, but not just for the marginalized. I kept meeting people who asked me the same question, and receiving letters from leaders and from Prison Fellowship members, and they all seemed to be saying the same thing: 'Most of the addicts we get in our church, or the men from prison, soon feel under condemnation due to their past, and we lose them. What can we do?' From within me came an unthinkable solution: 'Stop trying to lead them to where you think they should be, and help them work out where they are.'

There was a need for a discipleship environment wherein we all undergo the challenges of discipleship together. This would serve several purposes. It would create a sense of trust in the guy coming out of addiction and jail, who, up until conversion, had no concept of trust. It would create a sense of equality in this guy who is dying from the loneliness of an outcast. It would be a living application of Romans 3:23, 'for all have sinned and are falling short of God's glory'. It would be like us all climbing into a sheep-dip together, for sanctification and growth as one.

Chapter 11

The Society Wedding of the Year

Hope Now offered to pay for my dad's flight out to Cape Town for my wedding. I had considered inviting Hayley, but my heart held a concern that it might be a little too much for her to handle on her own. I told my dad what Hope Now had offered, and he was just speechless.

Slowly, over the last eight years, since he sat across the prison visiting table hearing me tell him I had become a Christian, he had witnessed a very obvious growth and maturity in me. I had previously made promise on top of promise about getting drug free, and time and time again I had let everyone down, right up until the heartbreaking moment for him when he disowned me as 'no longer his son'. His heart had been broken more than once too often, and he was left with no alternative but to walk out of my life. He was strong enough and wise enough to see that I was hell-bent on destroying my life, but refused to allow me to destroy his also. He let go of me, so deep was his love for me.

And now, he was getting ready to fly to South Africa to watch me get married to a beautiful Christian lady. In a wonderful moment of healing and reconciliation, Dad said something that, years before, I had given up all hope of ever hearing again. He said, 'That's my boy.' He was now able to trust me and he had lost his fear about me and my way of life

When God touches one life, all those closest to that life also get blessed. I do not believe that, because God saved me from the pit of sin and despair, he also saved my family. The Bible does not teach that. What it does say is that they (the unsaved) will be blessed by our salvation, in the sense of them sensing our sanctification (1 Cor. 7:14). Dad and, it must be said, the hearts of my brother and sister and extended family also, now held a new peace around Colin. Gone were the days when the phone rang and a shock of fear would pierce their hearts.

Then one day, I rang for a chat with my dad, and Maureen very bravely expressed a concern about Dad's health and his ability to fly so far. I asked my dad right out if he felt it would be wise. He conceded that it might not be beneficial to his health, and we therefore cancelled the idea. I said to him that I would rather see him at my anniversary than my wedding, and with that we agreed to leave it. At the end of that phone call, I reminded Dad of his promise not to die before I graduated from College, and he once again promised.

Our big day

My heart almost exploded when I saw what God had done on 14 April 2001. Deanna appeared on her dad's arm, walking towards me down the aisle of Meadowridge Baptist Church, just over one year after I gave my testimony at the very same altar. I felt like Adam must have felt when God presented Eve to him for the first time. I had never realized the symbolism of the father of the bride handing her over to the groom, until that moment. It was heavenly. This totally proud father, the ex-chief of police, was walking in my direction to give me his extremely beautiful daughter.

Andy Morris sat next to me as my best man. I had known God had a special place in my life for this man, but this exceeded everything I could have imagined. Before flying out for the wedding, Andy took me to purchase my wedding suit. It was actually said that we looked like brothers. Alan and Linda could not make it to the wedding – Alan would have been my first choice for best man – but it felt so right to have Andy, my Christian mentor and friend, to see me through this awesome time. Almost the whole of the Hope Now Board of Directors and their families came out for the wedding, and God made known what was meant when he had it written, 'Your love for one another will prove to the world that you are my disciples' (John 13:35, NLT). I had friends beyond measure. The outcast of the outcasts – once crushed by loneliness and a fear of the future – now surrounded by true friends.

The Revd Vic Jackopson married Deanna and me, and when it was asked, 'Who gives this woman to this man?' both of Deanna's parents stood. Holding hands, they tearfully said, 'We do.'

A fifty-strong black choir from the Langa township church, built by Hope Now, sang for us. They boomed out like only Africans can, and in tribal colours too.

It was awesome. A far cry from injecting drugs into my bloodstream in public toilets, or sitting on railway embankments weeping to myself in the middle of the night through hopelessness. From the church we went to the Vineyard Hotel in Cape Town's lavish Claremont district for the reception.

It was a perfect end to a perfect day. Vic pulled me to one side at the reception and asked me, 'How can a vagabond like you end up as groom at the society wedding of the year?' He was so right. Deanna's parents pulled out all the stops to make their daughter's wedding something extra-special. Not only had they brought her into the world and brought her up to be the lady she is; they gave her away in the most wonderful fashion. Not only so, they then gave us flight tickets from Cape Town to Greece as a wedding gift.

I had given my testimony at Ashley Baptist Church in the New Forest in Hampshire in my third year of college. Straight after the service, a lovely husband-and-wife team, Chris and Ginney Balchin, approached me. Ginney did most of the talking and she told me of a flat they had in the attic of their home, and they were wondering if I would like to live in it for the final year of my studies. I had seized this offer with both hands and moved in as soon as I could. On our return from honeymoon, Dee and I moved into the little flat at 14 Dilly Lane, and it became our first little nest together. Chris and Ginney gave me a lovely, warm, Christ-centred environment to come home to; and now the Lord had put in the last missing piece – Deanna.

I had May and June to go to complete four years of study, and one more assignment to complete in order to qualify for a BA Degree in Applied Theology. I was almost there, and Dad was still alive. I had had a prayer in my heart about Dad being alive to enjoy this very exciting chapter of my life. I knew that the Lord was going to be performing many wondrous works through my life, as he had already done, but completing college was something I felt to be really special for my dad. It was something tangible for him, which he could not rationalize or minimize.

I settled into my little study at 14 Dilly Lane, and set about my final assignments. Many of my peers were striving for academic excellence, and I'm sure some of them got it. The problem with that desire, though, is that it is impossible to satisfy it. At the start of my four years, I picked up on something one of the lecturers said. He simply said, 'Just answer the question, and you will answer the question.' I could not believe it was that simple. If I answered every question they put before me, whether my answer was theologically accurate or not, I would get a degree? Simply take note of what two scholars have already said about the same topic, comment on their differing views and then give my own view. Could it be that easy?

I had no idea that the academic world attached a lot of importance to the quality of one's degree and getting 'honours', bit I was not out for honours. Being there was honour enough for me. So I had relaxed quite early on in my studies and was now reaching the end intact.

I was in the process of praying about the future and the wonderful ministry I had seen unfold at Beth Rapha, when I got an email from the church in Cape Town, offering me the job of heading up the Beth Rapha Ministry. I felt the Lord desired that I should take it. I accepted.

Validation and ordination

I had very little idea about what it meant to be ordained. I thought that if one was not ordained by a specific denomination, then one was not truly ordained. In my heart I wanted to be ordained under the hands of Vic Jackopson and Hope Now, and there was also a yearning to have my first ministers from Minchinhampton Christian Fellowship involved. I loved these guys, and they had invested heavily into my growth. What no one knew, because he had requested that no one should know, was that one of my elders, Doug Horton, and his lovely Spirit-filled wife Dessie, had faithfully deposited £100 into my bank account every month for the four years of my studies. This couple, like many others in that period of my life, 'familied' me in every sense, and I know today that if ever I am within sixty miles of their home and do not visit, I will be in serious trouble!

I sent out invitations to Minchinhampton Christian Fellowship, inviting them to my ordination on Saturday afternoon, 30 June 2001. That morning was my year's valedictory service. Not only had my brother, sister-in-law, sister, brother-in-law, and two nieces turned up; my dad was there, and my step-mum. Then to top it all off, Deanna's mum and dad flew in from South Africa to share this very special day with us. This went way beyond reconciliation. It was reconciliation, restitution and remuneration. God had reconciled, restored and added on to everything that the dark years had sucked away from me. It went way beyond anything I would have asked for.

I had attended previous years' valedictory and graduation services, and to be honest, I found the valedictory service more meaningful. I thought the graduation service was more of an individual academic celebration, wearing what I thought were silly hats and cloaks. The valedictory service was more spiritual and a celebration of united completion. I felt extremely proud to be a part of that year group.

I now think it was quite symbolic that, in order for me to get onto the stage to collect the certificate, I would have had to do it all with my back to my family, facing the audience. I therefore went against the tide. I walked along the front of the stage in order to climb the steps at the opposite end to everyone else, yet facing my family. Cameras flashed and tears started to flow. This was very nearly the pinnacle of my family's joy at seeing their very own rebel without a clue, reborn and restored beyond measure to a life of respectability and health. The best, though, was yet to come. I left Moorlands College that day just as I had hoped four years earlier, with my dad, brother and sister tearfully celebrating what the Lord had done.

We were pushed for time, because the plan was to ordain me that same day, thirty miles away. At the church where I was to be ordained, a cheering Minchinhampton Christian Fellowship met us. It was awesome. I took a mortarboard hat and gown with me purely for a photo-session. Vic asked me to don the hat and gown. I went off stage to do this, and as I returned to the stage, Dessie Horton could not contain herself. She leaped to her feet and started to clap and yell, 'Praise the Lord! Praise the Lord! Praise the Lord!' It caught on, and within what seemed like seconds, the whole congregation were on their feet clapping and praising God for what he had done. It was so powerful.

I was simply staring at my dad as he sat weeping in the front row. He looked old and tired physically, but a fire of joy burned from deep inside him. We had eye-to-eye contact for a very long time wherein nothing was said, but everything was resolved. I think I knew what he was about to do before he did it, so I felt no surprise when he abandoned his walking-stick and stood very tall once again, his old back straight for the first time in years, and he strode up onto the stage, and to hell with etiquette.

Chapter 12

'That's My Boy!'

Dad limped up to me on the stage, in the midst of all the cheering, and he took my face in his big hands once again and said two things. He looked me right in the eyes and tearfully whispered, 'That's my boy!' He then said what I believe he had wanted to say more than anything else throughout all the years of sadness, and now he could say it: 'You know your mum would be so proud of you, don't you, son?' And we embraced. The applause went from extremely loud to ridiculously loud.

I was also very aware that, physically, Dad was just a shadow of the man he once had been, and the thought of the grave soon taking him crossed my mind. But now this worried me less, because he had seen God's power at first hand, and we were at one with each other.

We hugged and hugged and hugged.

Gary Fitzpatrick was there also. I had visited him every time I went back up to Stockport, and I had seen his addiction slowly but surely eating him away. I had always made a point of calling in on him, just to let him know that there was a way out if ever he wanted it. It was a year earlier that I went to visit him and found him in a suicidal state. He had actually written his note of goodbye to his mum and daughter and was at death's gate when I walked into his dark little basement flat in

Edgeley in Stockport. I saw deep sadness in his eyes. I said, 'Fitz, pack a bag and come with me to the south coast.' Within twelve hours we were southbound.

On the day of my ordination, Fitz was twelve months clean, and is now going on well on the south coast, drug free and working for a living. His daughter and her two sons have also moved to the south coast now, and Fitz regularly enjoys watching his grandchildren grow as he walks them by the sea. He recently told me that he bought his two grandsons their first bikes for Christmas, with honest money. When God turns a life around, he does so with such grace and kindness.

Back to Beth Rapha

Deanna and I flew back to Cape Town one week later and I went under the employ of St James' Church in Kenilworth, Cape Town. I immediately started working on a seven-step programme of recovery for drug addicts to follow, for establishing a new set of principles to live by.

I had told the chairman of the Beth Rapha board that I did not want to accept the house he was offering for Deanna and me to rent, because I did not think it would work for my landlord also to be my colleague. However, he wold not hear my 'no', and gave us a 50 per cent rent subsidy! So we moved into the house.

The work at Beth Rapha went from miracle to miracle. Men were saved and started to count drug-free days. I know from my own experience that recovery from long-term drug addiction is a long-term process, and I was reminded of something Charles Spurgeon once said about 'conversions': 'Refuse to celebrate overnight something that is going to have to undergo years of testing.' I watched with a hint of scepticism as men started to confess Jesus as Lord. I could see that some had been converted, and often cried before God for his mercy; but somewhere along the line, false light was also 'shining'. I was actually waiting for activity from forces of darkness, because I knew it would come.

One young man kept sabotaging the group sessions we held, by threatening to kill himself and devouring group time. He had made this threat several times to Malcolm before I arrived for this second time. He was holding the whole house emotionally hostage with his threats. He said it once in my group and I pinned his ears to the wall for ten minutes. I told him that if he made that threat once more he would be back on the street before the next lunchtime. That night he left and went back to using heroin. He made it look like it was my fault that he left. He was dead from a heroin overdose within a week. There was actually no evidence to suggest suicide, but the cruel reality of front-line ministry in the addiction field hit us all between the eyes.

The day the news came through about this young guy having died, I asked two more guys to leave the house for attempted mutiny. They went straight back to full-blown active addiction, and I started getting questioned by the board members and by the residents under my charge. But I knew from my own experience that a drug addict whose soul still belongs to addiction will stoop to the most extreme depths in order to make his or her drug use seem logical, by making it look like someone else's fault.

I felt like I was standing alone, but I knew I had to stand firm and continue in the vein that I had set out with: 'Get in line with the programme or get out.' This was the birth of a new ministry and we had to expect disruptions. Truth, grace and mercy were going to be the engine-room of this ministry, but it would have been extremely naïve to expect a smooth transition from it being a full-blown house of horror to a testimony of God's grace and a light in that dark place. I had witnessed P.J. McCullough and Wynne Parry, in both treatment clinics of my past, standing firm in their knowledge of addiction against irate and frustrated family members, and I expected the same. It came. Mums and girlfriends were demanding answers as to why I had evicted the loved ones they had also rejected.

We pressed on. Very slowly an attitude of change crept in. Day after day in the small-group setting, the men would start to express how they felt about themselves, their childhood, their parents or the lack of, their hopelessness and their despair about being drug addicts. We started to get real about our condition, and the Holy Spirit started to help us get real about who God is.

On the whole, we were dealing with heroin addicts. Addiction is addiction, and has its roots in sin, and the answer remains the same: surrender to the true and living God. But when it comes to ministering to heroin addicts, there seem to be more blocks to recovery than with addictive disorders involving other drugs. Heroin addicts have absolutely no pain threshold as they come off the drug. Heroin, in my opinion, could be referred to as the mother of hedonistic chemicals. It brings the ultimate in euphoric sensation. It does not harm the body, but steals the soul. The Hazleden Foundation states that heroin is the most pleasure-producing drug and its long-term use is not physically harmful. Damage issues concerning heroin are mainly connected to mis-use of the drug (overdose) and poor self-care (infection/malnutrition).

I gave the guys under my charge permission to forget about finding work, to forget about their broken marriages, and not to worry about funding for their stay and counselling. The only way a person can truly feel good about himself or herself is when they can look at themselves and see what God sees. That is the platform for salvation and it is the springboard into a healthy self-esteem. If an unregenerate person looks at his or her state of alienation from God, it can only serve to strike up the required state of humility. Then in the new birth, that same person should be at wonderful peace with who they are, knowing that they are so wonderfully loved from above.

My policy was that for a two-year period the guys should avoid major commitments, such as work and romantic relationships, for the purpose of stabilization. The number-one priority had to be their personal relationship with Jesus and learning how to live free from chemical dependency. Surrender to Christ is the end of the nightmare, but only the beginning of the war.

I was fortunate in that Jesus made himself alive to me in prison. I did not have the seduction of romance to contend with, and in the six months leading to my release, I only had the one option: to sink in depth of intimacy with Jesus. The Beth Rapha guys were really up against it. We were surrounded by prostitutes and drug merchants, so it was essential that we eradicate as many other snares as we could.

One of the neighbours opened his door for our guys to use his weights gym, and when I was told, my heart started to sink again. We were dealing with addicts, masters of self-avoidance and approval-seeking. If there was anything that would serve as avoidance of feeling any form of emotional pain, you could count on our guys to be first in the queue.

Brian

One guy in particular became a prime example of this.
Brian had crumbled in front of our very eyes during my
initial five-week period at Beth Rapha. He wept and fell
in love with Jesus. He grew physically and spiritually,
but my fear was that these were the only areas in which
he grew. When it came to social skills and assurances of
identity, I had no reason to believe that Brian had what
it took to stand or walk with integrity in community.

Our guys started to stand out in church. People started to notice how well they looked. I saw storm-clouds
gathering. I noticed that some of them would suddenly
stand up just before the service was about to start, and
they would move to another seat at the other end of the
church. Brian did this quite a lot. He was clean-looking
and physically growing. All outward signs said this was
a young man who was feeling good about who he was.

He was getting his identity and esteem from an exter-
nal stimulus. I had taken Brian under my wing and was
nurturing him for leadership, with the agreement of all
concerned. I challenged Brian that he might now be
using things like weights to 'improve himself', and that
a sure-fire sign of this would be that he would next be
involved in a romantic relationship. I detected a hint of
resistance in Brian towards this, confirming that it was
just a case of 'when', and not 'if', he relapsed. Sure
enough, Brian started seeing a lady from church. He
closed down to any form of feedback.

I put Brian out of Beth Rapha and back onto the street.
I told him to get on with the relapse and just prayed that it
would not kill him. The lady involved ended up getting
run through an emotional battlefield, including having
items stolen from her house and being convinced that it
was not Brian, right up until he started to use heroin again.

Brian ended up back in Pollsmoor Prison in Cape Town. His relapse progressed to him stealing from the collection plate and sleeping under a bridge each night. He put a note in the collection plate as it passed him, and then sat back and waited. Just before the ushers retired to the counting-room, he approached them and said, 'Please forgive me, I only meant to put 20 rands in the collection and by accident I put in 100. Can I have 80 rands change, please?'

I knew that he must be left to sink if need be, because until he saw that God was all he had, he would never realize that God was all he needed. It all began with a romantic relationship. The one thing that we each seem to crave so badly, seems to be the one area in which most damage is caused – and therein we have the clue.

It was not just a desire for a relationship; it was a craving. What rings in my ears is that Brian really believed that this was a relationship from God, because he said, 'We pray together.' Unfortunately, he had actually stopped weeping too soon, and drifted out of love with Jesus. Brian loved Jesus, and more importantly, Jesus loved Brian.

However, the Lord slipped from first position in Brian's heart to at least fourth. His priorities were: (1) the ego; (2) the weights; (3) romance; (4) Jesus Christ. Anything one puts before God, one will have to forfeit, to find God.

As the year unfolded, though, a great work was done in the hearts and minds of many who were close to death in addiction, and also in their families. We reached many, and witnessed a ministry of reconciliation. I knew that I had the wherewithal to do what the treatment clinics did. I also knew that, to exercise these talents under the government of discernment, grace, mercy and truth, would produce more fruit than Europe's finest secular attempts.

I felt it was time for me slowly to back away from Beth Rapha as the year came to an end, and felt the Lord would have me edge my way out over the next twelve months. I had worked myself out of a job. The committee had new plans and new visions for the future of Beth Rapha, and with that I felt safe to move on. I explained that they would have to do without me because I did not agree with the way they wanted to run the show, so it was best that we part company.

The men living at Beth Rapha and the new team of leaders sat me down and asked me to stick with them, or they would simply follow me. The love we felt for each other was extremely deep. We all felt that trying to run such a ministry under one specific denomination was not going to work.

When separation was suggested at the final committee meeting, the tension was tangible, but the change was made. The Beth Rapha Ministry went under an inter-denominational steering committee, and still is to this day.

It was truly humbling to see how God was speaking into the lives of addicts in my charge, by the way their lives changed and how their attitudes gradually went from negative to positive. I worked in and at Beth Rapha, five days a week, for over twelve months. I slowly started to feel like I was carrying up to fifteen men at one point, and their families. I was questioned day after day about Scripture and about living clean and paying one's way in life, and so on. Then the wives would be knocking at the door, wanting their husbands to suddenly have it all together and to start taking responsibility for the children. It was non-stop. But we managed.

My fears were that the ministry was resting on my shoulders rather than on the Lord. I often felt very important and very spiritual. To add to this, it seemed that every time anyone came with questions, it appeared that the Lord kept giving me answers that brought peace into many tormented souls. I knew it was God. It had to be, but many times I would sit and wonder how I was going to answer the next question. Very often I would hear the answer coming out of me, and I would often think to myself, 'I didn't know that I knew that.'

God was there every time. My struggle came in the area of pride and self-righteousness. I had to confess frequently the inner workings of my heart, and so I found God's peace. I find it amazing how negative feelings are just like negative photographs. They prosper in the dark, but simply die on exposure to the light.

Time to move on

On arrival at this place of peace, I increasingly felt that I was approaching the time to move on. The guys in positions of leadership were still quite vulnerable in their new lives, but strong enough, I felt, to carry on without me. Then one Friday morning, Malcolm and I sat in the office and prayed for another leader to come along. Up until this point it had been an all-white team, working in a mixed cultural setting. My fear was that we would fail to reach many if we did not cover the colour divide.

That afternoon, a coloured guy turned up with his holdall under his arm and simply said, 'The Lord wants me in here.' John Roberts, a guy from the drug culture with twenty years' clean time under his belt, joined the leadership of the Beth Rapha Ministry. I introduced John to the system and invited him to sit in on the group sessions for a month. John was blown away by the dynamic of the Beth Rapha group sessions. God showed up in wonderful ways each time we opened his Word.

At night, in our rented townhouse, Deanna and I would chat about the next leg of the journey. I started to express a desire for a pastoral position, even as an evangelist, because my entire ministry had been with gangsters and alcoholics. I longed for the little old lady who has just lost her cat, or the husband in need of guidance, or the teenager whose body was coming alive. I wanted regular ministry. I needed to know that I could reach everyday folk with everyday issues.

I contacted Vic back in the UK and this was also central to his heart for my next step in ministry. I left the employ of Beth Rapha and went back under Hope Now. Deanna and I put in an offer for a house in Fish Hoek, and within a week it had been accepted and we began to plan for the future. I approached King of Kings Baptist Church to ask if I could join their pastoral team, keeping the 'Evangelist' title, and they accepted us into fellowship with them with open arms. It felt really good to be in among relatively level-headed people. I set up my office in King of Kings, and started to pray about the exact direction the Lord would have me take next.

I became part of a team and found it extremely difficult. I'd gone from running the show, in among society's ragamuffins, to joining a team of middle-class straight-heads.[11] It was really weird, but really nice. At our induction I was introduced as being on the discipleship team, 'focusing mainly on the goats'. I now had an office to go to each day. I got what I asked for. People coming for counsel because of things like a death in the family, and for an alcoholic husband, son or daughter. Parents, who, in my opinion, had as many problems as the kids they were judging, brought wayward kids to me.

I was amazed. I'd gone from young men who had committed killings in the gang world, and from men who had been systematically raped by family members as children, to what looked to me like mundane issues, and yet I saw exactly the same depth of anguish in the sufferers. I was using all the same counselling techniques in a church-pastoral seat as I had at drug rehab, and people were receiving some wonderful healings. Men and women from 'Normal Street' were sobbing in my office over problems I might recently have seen as trivial. I had so much to learn.

Discipleship courses

During an early morning prayer time I sat in my study trying to seek definite direction for my talents. I started to feel a very strong pull towards the teachings of Dr Henry Cloud and Dr John Townsend. I had attended a Boundaries Course during the Beth Rapha period and I was amazed at how these guys had married psychology to theology.

The treatment clinics I had attended in my days of havoc were psychology-based, and had done an amazing job on and in me. They failed, however, to help me see the answer. They simply helped me see what the problem was, therefore keeping it alive. Cloud and Townsend tackled the psychology-versus-theology questions in me, and I suddenly found a teaching that scratched exactly where I itched. I could grasp that suffering and sickness is all rooted in sin, but could not find peace that suffering people simply had to repent for healing. I felt that was like asking a child to grow up. Not only is it impossible to turn growing up into an event, it is downright unfair and very damaging.

I found that Cloud and Townsend addressed my innermost developmental needs and the tasks that I was required to undertake in order to grow in maturity and healing. I tapped into www.cloudtownsend.com and looked at their list of video discipleship courses. I felt very strongly that I should use them.

I knew that God desired my healing, but I kept my broken parts hidden from the whole world, inwardly believing I could keep them hidden from God too. I was hiding from love. I needed to come out of hiding. Only then, in a place of spiritual, emotional and psychological safety, could I look at my past relationships, and myself, and learn how to make changes that would heal me. I knew that this was to be my next line of discipleship, for me as a child of God, and as a minister for God.

I wrote to Hope Now and asked for a series of Cloud and Townsend video discipleship courses. Within ten days, a parcel arrived from America containing the courses, and an added one for married couples.

Once again, everything made sense. Every lonely minute of the addiction made sense. Every hour-long-minute of every prison sentence made sense. Every minute spent in every one of the self-analysis groups in every rehabilitation environment all suddenly made sense. Every frustration I had felt with every brother and sister in Christ since my release from jail now also started to make sense. It was all for just such a time as this.

God had not only allowed it all, he had even guided me into and through it all. I had brought out of the world a distorted view of what Christianity was all about, and then, quite arrogantly, I had transferred extremely high expectations onto the church, based on my encounter with Jesus. I had set myself up for disappointment in the church, by expecting the church to be Jesus all the time, and expecting every sermon to be 'doctrinally accurate' from within my biblical understanding. I left no room for the opinions or views of others. I realized that I expected perfection.

Seeing this expectation as unresonable allowed me a new level of freedom and acceptance of others. Each of us is flawed by virtue of our humanity. It was the enemy of *my* soul that stirred me to be dissatisfied with *your* soul. It was the critical eye of perfectionism and my own personal dissatisfaction that drove me to desire biblical knowledge and wisdom. It was my finger of blame and resentment that stopped me looking at my own weaknesses, and it was my inner longing for belonging that fuelled my desire to give testimony everywhere I went. I failed to notice that even in the midst of what I thought was 'ministry', the enemy was slowly gaining ground within me.

My motives shocked me. I carried within me desires for perfection, beauty and wisdom. I wanted to be anointed and ordained so that I would have position, power and prestige. Walking in the light of the truth is such a difficult calling.

I began running Cloud and Townsend's 'Solution' courses in the church, starting with 'Hiding from Love'. I saw and personally experienced growth in a whole new way. I saw Christians opening up about homosexuality issues, and things like deep-seated hatred for spouses came to the surface. People started to heal, after years of believing that 'this is as good as it gets' – a condition I now call 'saved but stuck'. These guys jumped at the opportunity of doing more of the courses, becoming hungry for growth, and it was the eagerness of my brothers and sisters in Christ to grow that re-energized me for God.

Jesus said, 'Blessed are those who hunger and thirst for righteousness, for they shall be filled' (Matthew 5:6). I saw a new meaning to this text when his people started to weep over their sin and to release their secrets. I knew that I was at this place for another season for another reason, and as people wept in the small-group discipleship environment, I felt God's peace.

I once again noticed that, just like at Beth Rapha, people were hanging on every word I said, and often I was again surprised by what came out. For the sake of integrity, I decided to lead these courses in a threefold fashion. I led by example, by teaching and by limping. I led by example by testifying to the Lord's healing hand of mercy in my life; I led by teaching in exposition of God's Word at appropriate times and places; and I led by limping, in that I too underwent some exposure of flaw, and overcame the shame by receiving help from the people around me.

It became more and more apparent that God had placed quite a special anointing on my heart and mind. I was inclined to deny it by means of false humility, until the Lord showed me that true humility is accepting that we are who God says we are. It seemed to be one revelation after another since the day Jesus met this junkie in a trash can. I knelt before him and from deep within my heart offered him nothing but a broken heart, filthy hands and a whole armoury of selfish motives. From that moment, and right up to and including this day of writing, many years later, he has been and is filling my heart and life with good things.

Georgia Clare

Still on the payroll of Hope Now in Southampton, Deanna and I purchased a house in Fish Hoek, Cape Town. It was not on the side of a valley, as was dreamed of years ago. It was actually one step up from that. God knows my heart, and that if he gave me a home on one side of the valley, I would soon start to wish I lived on the other side. Our home sat upon a tiny hill, in the base of a valley, thereby giving us an all-round view of the valley, with the sea and the mountains to the front. God surpasses every desire and dream. He showers his children with grace upon grace, kindness upon kindness. Not only did that home consist of my wife and I, which would have been more than enough for me. We also shared it with our daughter Georgia, two Jack Russell dogs and two cats.

Georgia Claire was born after Deanna had undergone a whole night of discomfort and then five hours of extreme labour pains. I was reduced to a humble observer. It would be spiritually and biologically impossible for me to love Georgia any more than I love Hayley, but to see Georgia arrive through the sufferings of her mum really touched me deep inside. I was in jail when Hayley was born, and my celebrations were thwarted, so here again the Lord was restoring the blessings of life to me. I watched my wife transform into a mother right before my eyes, producing a new life that we had both planned and prayed for. The depth of love and respect that I felt for Dee intensified, and this new little life started to work her way into a new chamber of love within me.

Am I dreaming? Is this me? Was that junkie guy really me? The five and a half years in twenty-seven different prisons, the overdoses and rehabs – was it all real? It all seems like it happened to someone else, so radical was the change that took place within my heart. I have never experienced any desires to take up any form of drug use since the day I received my personal relationship with Jesus Christ, and there we have the key.

Throughout the writing of this book there have been many references to the concept of 'relationship'. It was in 'relationship' that all my pain was based, and it is in 'relationship' that the root of all restoration begins, even to the point of becoming a husband and a parent. I look at Georgia today, and realize that as she looks at me, she catches her first and lasting impressions of what God will be like to her as a heavenly Father concept. As she walks by my side, stretching up to grasp my little finger for stability, and as she somehow knows that she has my full approval, I see a delight in her eyes that the world will never offer her. I see the enormity of parental responsibility in that Deanna and I are the primary role models in her life, and we must therefore continually seek closeness to God ourselves, because really, she is his.

I am aware that there are in me secret desires for Georgia which could easily delay and even distract her from meeting with the Lord himself. I felt inclined to make up my mind, before she reached her first birthday, what she will do as a career and to even start saving toward her future at Veterinary School. In an attempt at being the parent, I think I should be as is laid down by the demands of the world and my past failures as a parent. I easily lose sight of the eternally important list of priorities. I forget that my personal relationship with Jesus Christ is the single most important example that I could ever set Georgia, because of her needs as a developing sinner separated from God. I truly believe that in the eyes of God, this is the most important lesson he would have her learn throughout her life: the need for salvation.

God willing, Georgia will have a long and fruitful life, and if I have done my job as her parent properly, she will see the reality of her own soul's need for a real, intimate and personal relationship with this Jesus, the Risen Son of God. All other relationships will then follow suit. What good is it if she wins the world and forfeits her soul? The greatest gift I could ever offer Georgia, or any of my children, is the truth of God's awesome grace towards sinners, offered in the life, death and resurrection of his Son Jesus. If I fulfil my parental role in a truly godly way, then Georgia will one day understand the need to bow her knee to him and receive promotion from being my daughter to being my sister in Christ.

The birth of a business plan

During this pastoral year, I started to see where God did *not* want me. I spent more time in my computer than I did in counselling. Day after day I would be looking at how and where we could have done things differently at Beth Rapha, knowing that we had the potential for birthing an internationally influential ministry, if only we had had an undivided heart amongst the leadership.

Very slowly, a business plan was born. If 'he who pays the piper calls the tune', why not start something that could pay for itself?

I visited a secular addiction treatment clinic in Cape Town, similar to the one I was sent to by the court and in which I had worked as a student. I felt an inner sense of indignation to discover that the price of a four-week programme was 25,000 rands. Yes, it is a wonderful programme including detoxification, medication and 24-hour nursing care, with very professional addictions counsellors. Not only so, it is becoming more and more popular for European addicts and/or alcoholics to fly to Cape Town for this treatment, because the prices in Europe are somewhere in the region of £19,000 per month. Therefore, in the typically worldly way, the price in South Africa is about to rise. I was extremely honoured to be offered a job by this specific clinic in South

Africa as an Addictions Counsellor. I informed Hope Now what I had in mind and I took the job on a three-month trial basis.

I drank a huge amount from their well of insights into what they call 'the disease of addiction'. At the end of the three-month trial period, I had to gratefully decline the offer of full-time employment. It was a trial period, but I was not on trial. They were. I declined on the grounds of me having to take the final piece of the jigsaw home every night with me, because the preaching of the gospel is forbidden. During that term of employment, I was devastated to see how many Christians were in there, paying these ridiculous prices, to get help from the world. The church of the living God, the pillar and foundation of truth in society, turning to the world for help?

I feared we were losing the war. I found that unacceptable. I had to do something. It was time to let go, sell our home, and step out onto the water.

Chapter 13

The Bethesda Christian Rehab

I spoke to Dee about a conviction in me that it was time to resign from Hope Now and to set out in a ministry within our own calling. We had bought our first house and made it a home. We were financially secure and to the outside world, ministerially happy.

In October 2004 I wrote to Hope Now and offered my resignation. Vic was waiting for it. It was agreed that I should leave Hope Now from 1 March 2005. Deanna and I felt the shake of insecurity because we had matured backwards into getting our security from third-party sources rather than directly from God. In a few months' time, it looked like I was going to be unemployed.

Family holiday

In December 2004 we agreed to take a holiday with Dee's family and get away from all the concerns of life for a few days. Because Georgia was still unable to climb stairs, we wanted somewhere safe for her to crawl about in.

Someone suggested a hunting lodge in Storms River Village, in the Tsitsikamma Forest. It sounded great, and on 27 December, we made the seven-hour trip to our holiday accommodation. On the way there, my brother-in-law Andrew asked, 'How would you feel about relocating to this area?' My heart changed pace.

When we arrived in Storms River Village and pulled up outside the hunting lodge – an extremely beautiful five-bedroom house sitting at the foot of Formosa Peak – I simply knew. 'This is it.'

Over supper that night, as we commented on the peace and beauty of the place, I dropped the following bombshell: 'This is where we are going to open a rehab.'

The conversation exploded about the place not being for sale, the high cost of property in that area, schooling for Georgia, and the logistics of it all.

'None of that is my problem. Those are all God's problems. I just know that the Name of Christ is going over that front door.'

The next day I phoned the owner of the property and the conversation went as follows:

'Hi, I'm staying at your property in Storms River and I was wondering, how much do you want for it?'

'It's not for sale.'

'I didn't ask you that. I asked you how much you want for it.'

'It has been valued at 1.6 million rands.'

'I will give you 1.6 million.'

'What?'

'I will give you 1.6 million rands. Let me rent the place from you for nine months, and then I will give you your asking price. If it's not a done deal by then, you get the place back and the place has been rented all year.'

'Starting when?'

'March the 1st, 2005.'

'Done.'

'I will rent it from you for nine months and then give you 1.6 million rands. But if I can make a concrete offer within four months, you sell it to me for 1.4 million. If it takes five months, 1.5 million. Between six and nine months, 1.6 million. Anything over nine months and you can name your own price.'

'Done. I will phone you tomorrow with a fee for the rent.'

As simple as that.

Dee frantically asked me, 'How can we be so sure that this is what the Lord wants?'

I said, 'I'm not so sure yet. We need to ask for three corresponding acts of providence. His name is Jehovah Provider. He will therefore provide.'

In my business plan, I had allowed for 10,000 rands per month for the rent of whatever property we found. I was expecting the rent to be 12,000 per month.

The landlord rang back the next day and said 7,000 rands per month.

That was one.

We enquired about accommodation for us as a family, not wanting to bring Georgia up in a rehab. We were told, 'My husband does all the rentals in Storms River and there is nothing going. There is one possibility, however. Go and ask the guy in the wooden cottage just down the lane.'

We knocked on the cottage door and I just said to the guy who opened it, 'We are Christians wanting to open a rehab in the village, but my wife, child and I need our own accommodation.' Slightly shocked, the guy invited us in and said, 'We are also Christians and we would really appreciate it if you guys rented from us. We only come here once a year, but we are not coming back now for a few years. How does 2,000 rands per month sound?'

That was two.

As we left the cottage, we both started to feel nervously excited. But I said to Dee, 'There is no point going any further, really, because we will need a doctor, and where are we going to find a doctor out here in the Tsitsikamma Forest?'

As we drove back to the accommodation, I noticed a 'Village Surgery'. I walked in and met the doctor.

'Hi, I'm Colin. My wife and I are thinking of opening a rehab in the village.'

'Oh, wonderful! I used to work in rehab but had to stand down because I did not agree with what was taking place in there.'

That was three, and Amen!

Deanna, who will be the first to admit that she does not do change at all well, simply said, 'How can we *not* do this?'

The next morning I got up at 5 a.m. and went to sit in our car. I sat there and sobbed. I just sobbed and sobbed.

I knew that this Jesus who met me in a trash can, was now about to surpass my wildest dreams about catching souls from addiction and presenting them with the gospel.

Within one month, we had put our house in Cape Town on the market and sold it for the asking price – twice the amount we paid.

We bought all the furniture that a nice home in Tsitsikamma would need. We stepped off the property market for Kingdom work, knowing God to be faithful. In mid February we loaded up and tearfully moved out. By 1 March 2005, twelve beds were made and the wait began.

At last – therapeutic theology

Within eighteen months of placing the name of Christ over the front door, Bethesda has simply blossomed. As a family we purchased the property. As a business we now have a fully professional staff profile:

- Colin Garnett (BA Applied Theology), Programme Director, Pastoral Addictions Counsellor
- Deanna Garnett (BA, LLB), Director of Administration and Finance
- One Senior Male Addictions Counsellor
- One Senior Female Addictions Counsellor
- Two Male Addictions Counsellors
- Three Medical Doctors
- One Clinical Psychologist
- Three State-Registered Nurses
- One Social Worker/Counsellor

Bethesda has also undergone extensive inspections and examinations by the Departments of Health and Social Development of South Africa and has been duly approved and officially registered to accommodate and minister to 16 addicts aged 18 and upwards.

Nine months into our ministry, Deanna and I received a phone call from Andrew, her brother in Cape Town. During street ministry, they came across a guy in a church doorway who was stinking and slowly dying. During one visit to his doorway, through lost and hungry eyes, he said to Drew, 'Do you know, I was once in a leadership position in a drug rehab called Beth Rapha.'

It was Brian. He had been on the streets for four years and his addiction had truly beaten the ego out of him.

He came to Bethesda with his own swarm of flies. I have since baptized a fully committed Brian.

Today, Brian wakes up each day just to sing praises to God before dawn. He has to go out into the garden so that others can sleep. He has had all addictions removed, including nicotine, and he is deeply in love with the Lord Jesus Christ and his Word. He has had every desire of his heart met by a God who answers every prayer – but never as we expect him to.

I sit and wonder how many Christians have drifted out of their divine calling because they refuse to trust God with their worldly possessions. His ways are so much higher than our ways and his thoughts are so much higher than our thoughts. Trust him. You may have seen within my story extreme similarities with yourself or someone you know and love. Even your dreams of a normal life with wife and family are all the same, but for some reason things are not falling into place for you at this time. Friends, please hear my heart. The same God has the same desires for every one of you.

He is the God of reconciliation and restoration. He is the God of family and relationship, and freedom. He reduces everything that is to nothing, in order to turn the things that are nothing into something. If you have written this Jesus off and thrown all your beliefs into the trash, then I hope my story has in some way explained why you cannot find peace. He is where you left him, waiting for you.

Maybe you are at the gateway of addiction, about to write Jesus off as liar or lunatic. You have that right and you have that power. Just do not let it kill you. No matter how low you may feel you have sunk, please remember – this junkie found Jesus in a trash can.

Endnotes

1. A 'beasting' was a torturous gym circuit, which you had to repeat until you cried.
2. A 'sorter' is a piece of cannabis for bedtime, just to help you relax.
3. A 'beast' is someone who sexually abuses children. One sex-offender was killed in the riot.
4. Some quick-thinking hustlers had T-shirts printed with 'Strangeways Burning' on the front.
5. By December 1991, the slopping out was gone, and the staff were more respectful in their approach.
6. See James 1:14–15.
7. Police informers.
8. Manchester.
9. Military sentences excluded.
10. A false name.
11. People who have never been involved in the chemical abuse/crime/prison lifestyle.

TAMING THE TIGER

Tony Anthony

with Angela Little

Tony Anthony knew no fear. Three-times World Kung Fu Champion, he was self-assured, powerful and at the pinnacle of his art. An extraordinary career awaited him. Working in the higher echelons of close protection security, he travelled the globe, guarding some of the world's wealthiest, most powerful and influential people.

This fast-paced, compelling and, at times, chilling account is Tony's deeply moving true story. More extraordinary than fantasy, more remarkable than fiction, this blockbusting read almost defies belief. With fascinating insight into China's martial arts, and the knife-edge adrenaline highs of the bodyguard lifestyle, it documents the personal tragedy that turned a 'disciple of enlightenment' into a bloodthirsty, violent man.

From the depths of hell in Cyprus's notorious Nicosia Central Prison, all might have been lost, but for the visits of a stranger . . .

ISBN: 978-1-86024-706-4

CONQUERING THE DRAGON

Kim Goh

'I put the gun to my head, closed my eyes and I pulled the trigger.' For Kim Goh, caught up in a tangle of gang culture and drugs, this was just one of many life-threatening situations.

A successful businessman by the age of eighteen, Kim Goh's violent pursuits and ability to con people kept him from settling in countries for long. From Thailand to Minorca, New York to Switzerland, his life became more chaotic and restless as he indulged in gambling, drugs, alcohol and sex. Climbing his way up the career ladder of a UK triad, Kim soon found that his volatile nature caused his behaviour to spiral out of control with devastating consequences.

A gripping tale of a man searching for meaning and of a God whose intervention is both dramatic and life changing.

ISBN: 978-1-86024-616-6

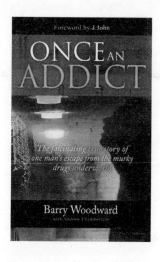

ONCE AN ADDICT

Barry Woodward

with Andrew Chamberlain

Barry Woodward was a drug dealer and heroin addict who once lived on the notorious Bull Rings estate in the centre of Manchester.

Once an Addict describes Barry's descent into the murky underworld of drug dealing, addiction, crime and imprisonment, and gives insight in to the city's nightlife and music scene, which was part of his world. Along the way we are introduced to some of the most extraordinary characters, and we see the extreme lengths to which some of them will go to get their next 'fix'.

Illegal drug use claimed the lives of many such people, and it seemed inevitable that Barry would also succumb to the drastic consequences of his addiction. With devastating amphetamine-induced mental health issues, a fourteen-year heroin addiction, a string of broken relationships, and the threat of HIV looming, the outlook for Barry appeared very bleak. Then three extraordinary encounters changed his life forever . . .

ISBN: 978-1-86024-602-9

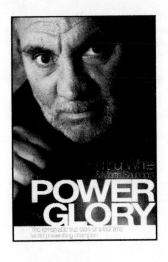

THE POWER AND THE GLORY

Arthur White

and Martin Saunders

Arthur White had it all. Not only was he a successful busi-nessman and happy family man – as a champion power lifter, he was literally on top of the world. But when he got to the top, he wasn't satisfied.

As he searched for a greater high, Arthur's life spiralled out of control. Drug addiction, an intense affair and a descent into violence followed, and before long death seemed like the only way out. As he stared into the abyss, an incredible encounter turned Arthur's life upside down. He would never be the same again . . .

ISBN: 978-1-86024-560-2